A Movement of Miracles

Books and booklets by Bill Bright:

A Movement of Miracles
Come Help Change the World
Revolution Now!
Ten Basic Steps Toward Christian Maturity
How to Be Sure You Are a Christian
How to Experience God's Love and Forgiveness
How to Walk in the Spirit
How to Witness in the Spirit
How to Be Filled with the Spirit
How to Introduce Others to Christ
How to Love by Faith
How to Pray
How to Help Fulfill the Great Commission
Have You Heard of the Four Spiritual Laws?
Have You Made the Wonderful Discovery of
     the Spirit-filled Life?
Paul Brown Letter
Van Dusen Letter

A Movement of Miracles

by BILL BRIGHT

Founder and President of Campus Crusade for Christ

CAMPUS CRUSADE FOR CHRIST INTERNATIONAL
San Bernardino, California 92414

Library of Congress Catalog No. 77 - 80071

ISBN 0-918956-38-2

Dedicated with deep gratitude,
thanksgiving and love to

OUR LORD AND SAVIOR JESUS CHRIST,
who is
transforming lives in an unprecedented worldwide
spiritual awakening in this generation.

And to all the Spirit-filled men and women
of His Church — many of whom participated
in Here's Life, America and continue
to be used of God to help make this
a movement of miracles in the lives of
millions of people.

Acknowledgments

I wish to express my profound thanks to God for the privilege of working with and my deepest personal gratitude to:

Bruce Cook, National Director of Here's Life, America, and Paul Eshleman, Co-Director, for their outstanding leadership;

Ron Blue, coordinator of Phase II for Here's Life;

Bob George, Sid Bruce and Tom Cummings who, along with Bruce Cook and Paul Eshleman, helped local pastors and laymen to develop the Here's Life, America pilot campaigns in the cities of Dallas, Nashville and Atlanta.

Our Field Staff, Pat Means, John Lynch, Glenn Plate, Loren Lillestrand, Roger Randall and Roger Vann, as they worked with our Regional Directors, Ron Blue, Dick Burr, Pat MacMillan, Jim Heiskell, Roy Box and Ralph Walls, for their contributions in helping to carry the movement nationwide;

Marvin Kehler, National Director, Campus Crusade for Christ in Canada, and his staff for the remarkable development and success of Here's Life, Canada.

Dr. Charles Stanley, Dr. Sam Coker, the Rev. Willie Richardson, Dr. W.A. Criswell and Dr. Howard Hendricks for their many messages of challenge and motivation in behalf of the Here's Life movement;

Dr. Billy Graham, for his encouragement, prayers and support in many ways;

Thousands of pastors and hundreds of thousands of lay men and women across the United States and Canada without whose leadership the Here's Life movement could never have succeeded on the local level;

Jim McKinney and his staff of Final Thrust, who helped provide financial counsel to the many Here's Life city campaign committees;

Chuck Younkman and his staff, whose Herculean effort provided the mediated training which is enabling us to train millions of Christians throughout the world in discipleship and evangelism;

Dr. Norman Bell and Bob Screen for their important roles as media consultants;

Bob Stark and his administrative staff, for the monumental achievement of supplying thousands of churches in hundreds of cities with the necessary training materials;

Thousands of Campus Crusade for Christ staff — from Headquarters, the Field Ministry and other ministries throughout the United States and Canada — who took temporary leave from other positions of major responsibility to serve pastors and lay people in each participating area;

Steve Douglass and his staff for their administrative counsel and leadership;

Our international staff and Directors of Affairs — Bailey Marks, Sergio Garcia, Don Meyers, Marvin Kehler, Gordon Klenck, Kundan Massey, Kalevi Lehtinen and Bud Hinkson — for their leadership roles for Here's Life, World;

The Campus Crusade for Christ Board of Directors for their dedicated counsel and leadership;

Erma Griswold, my administrative secretary, for helping to edit and polish the manuscript for this book;

Janet Kobobel for final editing of the manuscript, Judy Douglass for checking the typeset copy, and Bruce Johnson and his staff for design and production of the book;

Frank Allnutt, for long hours of research and assistance in compiling reports from Here's Life campaigns around the world, for editorial assistance with the manuscript and for overseeing publication of this book;

And last, but far from least, my beloved wife, Vonette, for her willing understanding of my traveling day and night most of the time during the past several years, meeting with Christian leaders and city fathers in as many as two and three cities a day, encouraging their involvement in Here's Life, America; and for providing leadership to the Great Commission Prayer Crusade, through which she has helped to mobilize tens of thousands of people to pray for revival in the United States, Canada and the world.

Preface

For nearly 2,000 years, the church has been spreading the good news of God's love and forgiveness through our Savior and Lord, Jesus Christ. However, it is this generation and this nation which God has chosen to bless with the wealth, technology and potential evangelistic task force for helping to reach the entire world with the gospel.

Now, in recognition of God's blessings, many committed Christians are praying and working toward the fulfillment of the Great Commission in this generation as a prelude to the blessed hope of Christ's return.

The Holy Spirit has empowered many individuals and movements to work toward accomplishing our Lord's Great Commission. Campus Crusade for Christ is one such movement. Thus, God gave this ministry the vision for developing a strategy — called Here's Life, America — to help equip the local churches for evangelism and discipleship in order to help saturate the world with the gospel by the end of 1980.

The local church from the outset has been central to the Here's Life movement. In fact, take away the local churches' participation and Here's Life would be a mere, impotent concept. But, because of the work of Spirit-filled men and women in many thousands of local churches, Here's Life has been called a movement of miracles.

A Movement of Miracles is the story of the Here's Life

movement and of how God worked in miraculous ways in the lives of dedicated pastors, committed lay people and those whose hearts responded to the good news of our Lord and received Him as Savior.

While Here's Life, America campaigns have officially come to an end in more than 200 participating cities, the spiritual awakening that grew out of these campaigns continues to be used of God to touch the lives of millions. Thus, the movement for which Here's Life provided the impetus is an ongoing movement — one that will reach its thrilling climax only when Jesus Christ returns!

It is my earnest prayer that each person who reads this book will be encouraged and enabled by the Holy Spirit to become more vitally and personally involved in helping the ongoing Here's Life movement and in helping to fulfill the Great Commission in this generation.

Bill Bright

Arrowhead Springs

Contents

1
Changed Lives

A retired Air Force brigadier general tells how he became a born again Christian through the Here's Life, America movement in Spokane, Washington.

A prostitute in Tucson, Arizona, turned her back on organized crime and began living a moral new life in Jesus Christ — the result of her response to an "I found it!" ad on TV.

A woman with terminal cancer prayed over the phone with a Here's Life trained layman in Indiana and received Christ as her Savior and Lord. That night she died and went to be with her new-found Savior.

A woman contemplating suicide in Dayton, Ohio, changed her mind and put her faith in Jesus Christ after a pastor working with Here's Life explained how she could discover a new life and hope in Jesus Christ.

From California to Maine, from Alaska to Florida, from Hawaii to Washington, D. C., and across Canada, hundreds of thousands — no doubt millions — of stories of changed lives resulting from Here's Life, America could be recorded. Though each is unique in its own peculiar set of circumstances, each testifies to the same life-changing experience which has resulted through receiving Jesus Christ as Savior and Lord.

A one-time seminary student who had never received Christ listened attentively as a young lady participating in

15

Here's Life, Anchorage, Alaska, shared with him the Four Spiritual Laws. He was so thrilled with the simple presentation of the good news of Jesus Christ that he immediately followed the young lady in a prayer and invited Christ into his heart.

A campaign worker in New York stopped by the central telephone center the night of the TV special. The 60 phone lines were tied up constantly with incoming calls from people who wanted to "find it," too. One of the phone workers finally wanted to take a break, so the "drop-in" filled in. On her third call a woman asked for the "I found it!" booklet, gave her name — and the campaign worker discovered it was her own mother! Only the night before, the campaign worker had prayed that her mother, who was not a Christian, would watch the TV special and receive Christ.

Each one had believed, had repented, and had responded to the promise of Jesus: "Behold, I stand at the door, and knock: if any man hear My voice, and open the door, I will come in to him" (Revelation 3:20, KJV), and "But as many as received Him, to them gave He power to become the sons of God" (John 1:12, KJV).

Hundreds of thousands — some would say millions — of men and women, boys and girls from all across America and Canada are finding a new life in Jesus Christ. The Bible tells us, "If any man be in Christ, he is a new creature" (II Corinthians 5:17, KJV).

"Greatest Impact on My Life"

Throughout the many cities which are participants in the Here's Life movement, pastors and church leaders are amazed and encouraged by the enthusiasm of their congregations.

"The greatest impact on my life was seeing new Christians win others to Jesus Christ," says Tim Roland, Christian education coordinator at Memorial Baptist Church in Fresno, California. "One Wednesday night at the Here's Life telephone center, a woman who had been a Christian only a few months was able because of Here's Life training to pray with four people who received Christ. The next

16

As Christians turned ordinary life situations into witnessing opportunities, thousands of churches saw enthusiasm swell and attendance increase.

Wednesday night she prayed with three more who received Christ. It excited her, it excited her husband, and it did a whole lot for our church."

Even children have become involved in spreading the message of Christ's salvation through faith. A first grade teacher in the Dallas inner city area shared the "I found it!" booklet with her class, then encouraged the children to take the books home to their parents. During class the following day, one little girl announced, "My Mommy and Daddy listened to me as I shared about Jesus. They both prayed with me and asked Jesus to come into their hearts."

Impact on Local Churches

Commenting on the results of Here's Life, America, William C. Ankerberg, pastor of Calvary Baptist Church in Kewanee, Illinois, said, "Perhaps the biggest change has been in the lives of our people. Our Sunday evening attendance has increased. God is good. The Here's Life program is a good tool, and our church has received blessings in these past few months."

The Rev. Bob Mowrey, pastor of the Park Avenue Baptist Church in Nashville, Tennessee, enthusiastically described the success of Here's Life in his church and community: "We participated in Here's Life, Nashville and had a very fine experience," he reported. "At least 15 of our workers won someone for Christ. We also found another 50 or 60 prospective families through work done with Here's Life, Nashville. Jim Heiskell of the Campus Crusade staff helped us to organize a core group of 12 men and train them for a year and a half in evangelism. All the men became fine personal witnesses for Christ. Two are now engaged in their own groups involving 35 to 50 people and are training them in evangelism and discipleship."

"I saw lives changed, I witnessed ministers and laymen blending their dreams and their faith as they sought to claim a city for God," observed Dr. Sam Coker, pastor of Grace United Methodist Church in Atlanta, Georgia. "This swept across the nation. I saw denominational barriers broken down, doctrinal differences disappear and people motivated by the Spirit of God to train and

18

equip themselves to reach out with the gospel and the love of Christ and invite people to receive Christ as the Lord of life.

"I have no statistics. I can't tell you how many souls were saved in the total effort. I only know that something happened in the lives of people I met and even in my own," said Dr. Coker. "A renewed vision of the commandment of Christ became a contemporary challenge for our turbulent times. Campus Crusade for Christ is a part of God's plan, and I believe He used the know-how, the materials and the vision of this organization to motivate churches and people within fellowships to work together to win our land for God."

Pastor Richard Emmons of Leptondale Bible Church in Newburgh, New York, reported that as a result of Here's Life, America, 26 follow-up Bible studies have become part of his church and that several more are being formed. Another New York pastor, Terrance Smith of the Mount Vernon Alliance Church, has seen regular attendance increase from 45 people to 100 as a result of Here's Life, America.

In the Hispanic community of New York, 58 Spanish-speaking churches took part in Here's Life, and God did amazing things within their congregations. One little Spanish church that was about to have to close its doors installed four telephone lines and during the first week of the campaign saw 44 people indicate they had come to know Jesus Christ. A storefront church had 24 new visitors one Sunday and began 13 Bible studies as a result of Here's Life. And one Brooklyn church member proclaimed of her involvement in the campaign, "The Lord has used me more in two days than in all the 12 years I've known Him."

United for Christ

Under the leadership of Jerry Regier more than 200 pastors in Washington, D. C., came together to pray and work toward the same goal — that of reaching their city with the good news of Jesus Christ. Bob Schneider, follow-up coordinator for Here's Life in Washington, D. C., marvels at what happened there: "It's the first time in history something like this has ever happened in Washington, D. C. That something like this could happen was beyond our wildest dreams."

God has been working repeatedly in the hearts of thousands of pastors in more than 200 major metropolitan areas throughout the country, impressing upon them the urgency and importance of taking seriously our Lord's Great Commission: "Go ye therefore, and teach all nations, baptizing them in the name of the Father, and of the Son, and of the Holy Ghost: Teaching them to observe all things whatsoever I have commanded you" (Matthew 28:19,20, KJV).

Denominational barriers have come down, church rivalry, prejudices and differences have been pushed aside for the common purpose of reaching entire cities for Christ.

Without the dedicated work of local churches from virtually every denomination, from the large metropolitan areas to thousands of the smaller townships and hamlets, Here's Life, America would not have become the life-changing movement that it is today. For, from the very inception of Here's Life, America, the local church has been central in implementing this movement.

Dr. W.A. Criswell, pastor of the famous First Baptist Church of Dallas, Texas, observed, "Campus Crusade for Christ gave great leadership and maintained a very low profile. It is a church movement with pastor leadership."

One of the most encouraging aspects of Here's Life, America is the fact that this ministry has the privilege of working with and helping to train hundreds of thousands of Christians from 14,000 churches of all denominations in more than 200 major cities and thousands of smaller communities across the nation. The continued excitement of many thousands of pastors and lay people over the miracles of this movement is evident.

Thousands of laymen, in faithful obedience to our Lord's Great Commission, are introducing others to Christ for the first time in their lives. Many churches are continuing to experience true spiritual awakening and harvest. The sheer magnitude of the Here's Life, America movement is overwhelming!

Yet, it is each individually changed life that matters, because it is the individual for whom Christ died. But if we rejoice over one person coming to Christ, we should rejoice much more when millions crown Him as their Savior and Lord.

One of the most important lessons that we have learned is that multitudes have been prepared by the Holy Spirit to receive Jesus Christ as Savior and Lord. What God is doing in the United States and Canada will, by the grace of God, soon be happening in every community and country of the world. Hundreds of millions will be introduced to Christ. To Him be all the honor, glory, worship and praise.

2
Urgency of the Hour

Here's Life, America was born out of one of the gravest periods of crisis ever to confront our nation, the late 1960's and early 70's. Never had there been such conflict in America since the days of the Civil War.

The black and white and Hispanic racial tensions burst into controversy, then open hostility. Crime skyrocketed 300% within a period of only a few years. Juvenile delinquency grew threefold. The controversy over the war in Vietnam was dividing our nation. A radical student movement was seeking to overthrow our government. The drug culture was on its ascendancy, and many millions of Americans were enslaved in the bondage of alcohol and drugs.

A sex revolution threatened the sanctity of marriage. The homes of millions of Americans were disintegrating. By the mid-1970's, in Washington, D. C., it was reported that there were more legal abortions performed than there were live births; our nation's capital was setting the pace for the rest of the country. There was disagreement between parents and children — estrangement that tore families apart.

So great had the crisis in America become that two of our Presidents were literally forced from their position of leadership of the nation. There was so much antagonism toward President Lyndon Johnson's role in the Vietnam crisis that his chances of being reelected were estimated to be very small. Consequently, he stepped down from the leadership of the Democratic Party.

Then came the scandal of Watergate — which was a product of this crisis — and President Richard M. Nixon was forced to resign the presidency, becoming the first chief executive in our nation's history ever to do so.

Disastrous Consequences

I believe that these crises were in great part the disastrous consequences brought about when our nation officially turned its back on God and rejected the importance of the Bible and prayer in our schools. I am referring to the 1962 Supreme Court ruling on prayer in public schools. That somewhat ambiguously worded ruling was interpreted by many school officials to mean that it was no longer legal to read the Bible and pray in our schools.

We are reminded in reading Deuteronomy, chapters 8 and 28, that whenever the people of Israel disobeyed God, He punished them; when they obeyed, He blessed. These same principles — commands and promises — from God's Word also apply to America, especially in light of our rich Judeo-Christian heritage.

So, when we as a nation took the official position that there is no place for God in the schools, we rightfully incurred the displeasure of God. And, immediately, the chastening of God came upon our nation like an avalanche.

A Warning from the Past

The words from Plato's *Republic* (4 B.C.) echo an ominous warning for the people of America:

"The citizens . . . chafe impatiently at the least touch of authority, and at length . . . they cease to care even for the laws, written or unwritten . . . and this is the fair and glorious beginning out of which springs tyranny . . . The excessive increase of anything often causes a reaction in the opposite direction . . . Tyranny naturally arises out of democracy, and the most aggravated form of tyranny and slavery out of the most extreme form of liberty."

Modern thinkers, addressing the condition of our society, reached conclusions similar to Plato's. In March 1977, a number of distinguished scholars and statesmen, including former Secretary of State Dean Rusk and former British Prime Minister Lord Hume, gathered at the Center for Study of the American Experience at the University of Southern California for a conference called The Future of the West.

One of the delegates, French author and scholar Jean Gimpel, asked, "Is the cycle which has been observed previously in other civilizations and cultures — that of ascension, followed by stability and dominance, concluding with disruption and decline — inevitable for the current society in governing structures of the West?" He answered his own question: "It is inevitable."

This view is widely held today by many leaders throughout the world and was especially popular during the turbulent '60's and early '70's.

Even today there is much confusion and conflict in the world. It is no exaggeration to say that the whole world scene continues to become more and more critical. From the human perspective there is more reason to be distressed, more reason to be concerned, more reason to believe that there is no hope for peace and for civilization as we know it to continue. Every day brings us closer to the brink of disaster. Our nation, indeed the whole world, has been largely leaderless, without goals or even power to achieve goals or direction. The entire world is like a giant ocean liner without power or rudders tossed by a great storm at sea, floundering helplessly out of control.

Time Is Running Out

Apart from a mighty movement of God's Spirit, civilization as we know it will soon cease to exist and the freedoms which we now enjoy in this great country and in a few other countries will soon be wrested from us by atheistic forces. What has happened in the Soviet Union, China, Eastern Europe, Vietnam and Cambodia, and what is happening on the African continent today, could well take place in the halls of government and homes of

America in this decade.

The tides of militant atheism are threatening to engulf the entire world. Many of our leaders believe that the crisis in the Middle East could well invite a coup by those who are indifferent to or militantly opposed to God and His rule in the affairs of men and nations. The threat is worldwide: Latin America, Europe, Asia, Africa, the Middle East, and even the United States, are all increasingly influenced and dominated by those atheistic forces.

Alexandr Solzhenitsyn, Nobel Prize-winning Russian author, warning of the growing Soviet military superiority, said in the March 15, 1976 issue of the *U.S. News and World Report:* "I wouldn't be surprised at the sudden and imminent fall of the West . . . The West is on the verge of a collapse created by its own hands."

Malcolm Muggeridge, one of Europe's leading intellectuals and authorities on worldwide communism, recently stated that in his opinion we have already entered the second Dark Age.

Francis A. Schaeffer, theologian and philosopher and one of the foremost evangelical thinkers of our day, writes in *How Should We Then Live?*: "Overwhelming pressures . . . are progressively preparing modern people to accept a manipulative, authoritarian government. Unhappily, many of these pressures are upon us now."

Dr. Schaeffer defines these pressures as: economic breakdown; war or the serious threat of war; the chaos of violence — especially random or political violence and indiscriminate terrorism, in an individual nation or in the world; the radical redistribution of the wealth of the world; a growing shortage of food and other natural resources in the world.

The Alternative in Christ

Dr. Schaeffer reminds us that there are only two alternatives in the natural flow of events: "First, imposed order or, second, our society once again affirming that base which gave freedom without chaos in the first place — God's revelation in the Bible and His revelation through Christ."

I agree that the only desirable alternative is God's alternative in Jesus Christ. Many people in our society are desperately searching for answers to our political, social, economic and military problems.

"New international institutions" and a "comprehensive and enforceable body of international law" are discussed at conferences such as USC's The Future of the West. Men blindly continue to count on finding solutions within themselves for the problems that face the world.

"What gives man uniqueness in the animal kingdom is his ability to do things for the first time," declared Norman Cousins, editor of the *Saturday Review,* at the Future of the West. But history offers no encouragement for man to become his own savior. The only hope is in the person of Jesus Christ.

"I am come," declared Jesus, "that they might have life, and that they might have it more abundantly" (John 10:10, KJV).

And it is at this moment in history, when man searches in vain for healing balms for his crumbling world, that Here's Life, America is born, with the express purpose of proclaiming to the needy world that abundance of life is in Jesus Christ.

The Importance of North America

But why the emphasis on America? Is not all the world in need?

Because God has uniquely blessed the United States and Canada with vast resources for reaching the rest of the world with the gospel. Americans have more money, manpower and technology than all the rest of the world put together to help fulfill the Great Commission. Those resources must not be misused or lost through neglect and apathy; our freedom to use those resources to further the cause of Christ must be preserved and used for His glory.

Obviously, there are many things about the United States that need to be changed. I am interested in helping to save this country not only because I love it as my home, where I was born and reared, but more importantly, I pray that our nation will be preserved in order to use our vast resources to help present the good news of our Savior and Lord to the world. I pray that that which is displeasing to God will be purged from our land, that we as a nation might experience a new birth of faith and freedom.

But we, as individual Christians, are the ones who will determine whether or not we, as a nation, will fulfill our God-given role in history. We have the option of claiming the promise God gave to Solomon centuries ago: "If My people, which are called by My name, shall humble themselves, and pray, and seek My face, and turn from their wicked ways; then will I hear from heaven, and will forgive their sin, and will heal their land" (II Chronicles 7:14, KJV).

We need to keep on believing, keep on humbling ourselves and keep on turning from all those sinful ways that hinder the working of the Holy Spirit. We need to keep on praying.

3
Rebirth of a Nation

Throughout the centuries, God, in answer to the prayers of His people, has shaped the destinies of men and of nations. The greatest power in the world is not military power, nor the power of money, nor the power of brilliant and gifted personalities. It is God's supernatural power — power released in answer to the believing prayers of obedient children of God (Psalms 116:1,2).

Several times in the history of Christianity the joyful news of Jesus Christ has so saturated an area that entire societies have been transformed. It has happened before and it is happening again — because millions of people are beginning to believe and obey God!

The first time was on the day of Pentecost, nearly 2,000 years ago, when 3,000 people cried out, "What must we do to be saved?" (Acts 2:14-41). For the next 300 years, Christians grew in number and the gospel of Jesus Christ spread throughout the known world. But this remarkable movement of God's Spirit was followed by a thousand-year period known as the Dark Ages.

On October 31, 1517, Martin Luther nailed his 95 theses to the door of Wittenberg Palace Church, and the Reformation was born. Once again, searching hearts responded to the joyful proclamation of the love of God expressed through His only begotten Son. And *light* dispelled the darkness. "God is light and in Him there is no darkness at all" (I John 1:5,NAS).

But the movement of God's Spirit during the Reformation was countered by the age of skepticism. Thus, two more centuries were to pass before the great Wesleyan Revival, led by John and Charles Wesley, would reach hundreds of thousands and ultimately millions of people throughout the world. But this mighty movement of God's Spirit was hindered in its spread by a movement of materialism.

Over and over again, through the centuries, Jesus Christ has become the issue in society. But each time the spiritual victory has been followed by an attack of Satan as he has offered to man his counterfeit religions. Men soon lost sight of God and denied themselves of His blessings. They disobeyed His command to make disciples of all nations. Instead, man has come to rely increasingly on humanistic philosophies, or his own knowledge, his own technical skill and his own material comforts.

But all these have failed to fill the gnawing emptiness inside. In his search for meaning and purpose, mankind has sought to fill what Pascal called a "God-shaped vacuum" in the heart of man with the warm stupor of alcohol, the ethereal dream world of drugs, the momentary passions of sexual immorality and the consuming desire for wealth, possessions and power.

Yet, all of these have been as fleeting as the morning dew. All have *failed* to bring lasting joy and peace; all have failed to bring purpose and meaning to life. The basic questions of life — "Who am I?" "Why am I here?" "Where am I going?" — remain unanswered for the multitudes who are crying out for help.

Thus in the emptiness of his soul, man has turned, once again, toward God. From the human perspective, man has no hope. But from a divine perspective, there is a *great* hope — in the person of Jesus Christ. Such hope is now sweeping across the continent of North America.

America's Spiritual Awakening

Today, God is responding to the faithful prayers of His children: America is experiencing a new spiritual awakening. For example, according to a recent Gallup poll, 85 million people in the United States attend church each Sunday, and one in five is involved in either a Bible study or prayer group each week in addition to their Sunday worship. Dr. Ben Armstrong, executive secretary of National Religious Broadcasters, reports that 125 million people listen to religious broadcasts each week.

According to "The Church Around the World," "More Americans went to church in 1976 than in any time since 1958, reversing an 18-year decline. 42% of the population attended church or synagogue regularly. The 1958 figure was 49%."

A recent *New York Times* headline read, "'Religious Revival' Forecast by Gallup: Pollster Finds Evangelicals Have 'Energized' the Movement." The story followed: "George Gallup, Jr., said last week that the United States 'may be in an early stage of a profound religious revival.' Mr. Gallup said theologians would describe evangelicals as persons who 'emphasize salvation by faith and the atoning death of Jesus Christ through personal conversion, the authority of Scripture and the importance of preaching as contrasted with ritual.'

"Paul H. Sherry, editor of The Journal of Current Social Issues, agreed with Mr. Gallup: 'A number of churches are reporting increased attendance at worship, people in our churches are pressing us to help them deal more effectively with questions as to the ultimate meaning of their lives, persons who seemed embarrassed about discussing religion are now openly expressing their feelings about God and their own religious movements are springing up everywhere. And the fact that President Carter is a devoted Christian probably contributes significantly to the new move.'"

Quoting from an as yet unpublished Gallup survey, Mr. Gallup reported that 6 out of 10 persons interviewed were favorably impressed with evangelicals and, for the most part, described them as devout, God-fearing persons.

In a survey of "Importance of Religious Beliefs in the United States," the Gallup poll stated that 56% of the American people indicated that their personal religious beliefs were "very important." This is in dramatic contrast to the Gallup survey results in 1970 which indicated that only 17% of Americans considered their religious convictions to be "very important."

Thus, the Gallup poll would seem to conclude that during the intervening six years a great spiritual awakening has been accelerating throughout America.

Another important indicator — a survey of 65,000 women in America taken by Redbook — revealed that 74% of those surveyed know God really exists and have no doubts about it. The results of this survey, which were reported in the April 1977 issue of the magazine, also showed that 73% of those surveyed approved of restoring prayer in public schools. Twenty-two percent attended more than one religious service a week. Thus, the Redbook survey confirmed the Gallup poll report that a spiritual awakening has indeed come upon the United States.

"Born Again"

During the past two years there has developed what might prove to be the greatest awareness of the gospel in the nation's history. Contributing to this was the dramatic way in which God raised up two Christian men to become the most popular candidates for the nation's presidency: President Gerald Ford — seeking his first elected term of office — was the Republican nominee, and former Georgia Governor Jimmy Carter was chosen by the Democratic Party. The secular press quickly emphasized the fact that both men professed to be "born again" Christians, then tried to define the phrase.

It was during this time that Charles Colson, legal counsel to former President Richard Nixon, published his story, Born Again, in the best-seller explaining how he found a new life in Christ.

Soon, the whole nation was aware that being born again meant receiving Jesus Christ as personal Savior and Lord. A Gallup poll indicated that 50 million people above the age of 18 years claimed to be born again — and it could well be that another 25 million below the age of 18 would also identify themselves as born again Christians.

Something was happening in America. The Holy Spirit was working in lives. God was answering the prayers of many of His people who were claiming the promise of II Chronicles 7:14.

A Strategy Is Needed

Beginning in 1974, God began to impress upon the hearts of the leadership of Campus Crusade for Christ that there needed to be specific national strategy to help saturate our country with the good news of our Lord. The pastors and lay leaders of the local churches of America were invited to give leadership in a great united thrust to reach our nation with the gospel. By the grace of God and the enabling of His Holy Spirit, this strategy has now become a reality. By the spring of 1977, the strategy which was developed — Here's Life, America — had been implemented in more than 200 major cities, was influencing thousands of smaller communities and had communicated the gospel to some 85% of all Americans!

As a result, we have every reason to believe that literally millions of people have made commitments to Christ though it would be impossible to document all or even a small part of this great miracle of God's grace. We do know, however, that more than 325,000 people from 14,-000 churches in more than 200 major metropolitan areas have been trained for evangelism and discipleship as of the writing of this book. And the best is yet to come!

History's Final Thrust

A spiritual awakening is indeed sweeping the country — and the world — perhaps for the last time. Fanned by the fresh wind of the Holy Spirit, a new search for eternal truth has been kindled in the hearts of men. In every country of the world, under every conceivable condition, the Holy Spirit is at work today. He is convicting men of their sins, filling their lives with love, peace and the power to be different. And He is offering to all people God's free gift of eternal life through our Lord Jesus Christ.

More individuals than ever before are hearing the gospel of Jesus Christ, and more people than ever before are responding to His invitation to a new life of fulfillment and abundance — a life everlasting. At this same time, more people are training to serve our Lord than ever before since the Great Commission was given almost 2,000 years ago.

And never before has the world been so ready to hear the good news of Jesus Christ.

A Call To Commitment

Sadly, however, revival has not reached its optimum potential. This is because some Christians have two great problems: lethargy and tunnel vision. Many Christians throughout the world are seemingly unaware of or are passive about the alarming events of our time. Other Christians are saying, "There is nothing that can be done. It is too late. The tide of atheism is running too strongly against us. We interpret all of the problems and tragedies of our time as the prelude to the imminent return of our Lord." There is a tendency for Christians to simply fold their hands and pray, "Lord Jesus, come quickly."

I don't believe that this is what God wants us to do. Indeed, we must follow our Lord's command to work as long as it is day, because night is coming, when no one can work (John 9:4). Furthermore, there are many Christians who are serving our Lord with great zeal in their local communities, but are concerned only with their local communities. They seem to have forgotten that we have been called to take the gospel to the entire world.

The world is our parish. We are to begin in Jerusalem, and from there go to Judea and Samaria and to the uttermost parts of the world (Acts 1:8). It is time for Christians to unite — not denominationally, not even perhaps on fine points of doctrine, but to unite in a common thrust to carry the gospel throughout the world. "And then," as Jesus foretold, "the end will come" (Matthew 24:14).

Remember that the one behind the crisis we face in the world today is none other than Satan himself. He is the enemy of our souls. He uses and deceives men and nations. But remember, too, because of the cross and empty tomb our Savior has overcome Satan and his agents. We

33

have this thrilling assurance from God's Word that "the one who is in (us) is greater than the one who is in the world" (I John 4:4, NIV).

God's promise is still true: "If . . . My people, who are called by My name, will humble themselves and pray and seek My face, and turn from their wicked ways, then I will hear from heaven and forgive their sin and heal their land" (II Chronicles 7:14).

The World Is Changing

I believe we will see our world change. I believe that the spiritual awakening that is sweeping North America will soon be sweeping Russia and China and every country of the world. I believe that the awakening that is sweeping our nations will soon affect our educational institutions, the electronic media, the press, the entertainment world, our homes and our churches. I believe that we are going to see in the near future an acceleration of all that has now begun and that within the next few years there will literally be a revolutionary spiritual impact upon our nations and from our nations on the whole world.

I am not saying that man will build a utopian world through his own ability. Society will change as individuals in large numbers change. The ultimate change will take place when our Lord returns to this earth to establish His kingdom. There will be no lasting peace — no utopia — in this world until the Prince of Peace rules in the hearts of men and nations.

4
From Vision to Reality

Dr. Charles Stanley, pastor of the First Baptist Church in Atlanta, Georgia, and his wife, Anna, were having lunch in the revolving restaurant atop the Regency Hyatt House overlooking the city, when God began to impress upon him a vision for reaching the people of the city with the gospel of Jesus Christ.

As the restaurant slowly revolved, Dr. Stanley sensed that God was speaking to him. "I began to get a new glimpse of the city of Atlanta," he recalled. "I began to see it from a whole different perspective." He thought, "We, of the First Baptist Church, are responsible for reaching this city for Jesus Christ."

Soon Dr. Stanley began to talk to others about the vision God was revealing to him. Though the First Baptist Church had two weekly television programs, a vast bus ministry and many other outreaches in the city, God was telling Dr. Stanley there was more to be done.

A Growing Concern

Realizing the tremendous challenge of reaching Atlanta's 1.6 million people for Christ, Dr. Stanley recalled praying, "Lord, there is no way, personally, for me to reach this city. There's just no way to do it. I'm just one man — there are a lot of other churches here and maybe we could somehow all get together." As the burden grew in

Atlanta successfully launched the Here's Life movement with "Agape Atlanta."

Atlanta's vision spread to different cities, but the message stayed the same: "I found it!"

his heart, Dr. Stanley asked our Lord to show him what he could do about reaching the city of Atlanta for Christ.

At the same time God had placed an unusual concern for the city of Atlanta on the heart of Cobby Ware, an all-American golfer and an ordained Presbyterian minister, who was then director of Campus Crusade in the Atlanta area. He was so deeply concerned for his city that he called me at Arrowhead Springs where I was meeting for prayer and planning that very day with several of our Campus Crusade leaders. We were asking God for a strategy to help our nation's local churches saturate their cities for our Lord.

As Cobby shared his burden, the sparks of excitement and enthusiasm literally exploded! We had been asking the Lord to direct us to the right cities to develop pilot projects from which what was to become Here's Life, America would expand throughout the nation. Immediately we knew that Atlanta was to be one of those cities. Later we added the cities of Dallas, Texas, and Nashville, Tennessee.

Bob George — a successful businessman who, together with his wife, Amy, had received Christ during one of our TV programs, joined the Campus Crusade staff. Later, he was asked to move to Dallas to give leadership in developing the saturation strategy in that city.

Their counterparts in Nashville were Col. Sid Bruce and his wife, Jean. Sid had recently retired from a brilliant military career.

The Atlanta project was headed by Bruce Cook, a graduate of Georgia Tech and Harvard Business School who was my assistant for special projects. Bruce and his wife, Donna, moved to Atlanta from California to help Cobby Ware and the other Christians of many local churches reach their city for Christ.

The Vision Confirmed

Within days Bruce Cook and Cobby Ware met with Dr. Stanley — unaware that God had already prepared his heart. They shared with him that God had impressed upon the leadership of this ministry to assist and serve the pastors and local churches of America in a great movement to share the gospel with our entire nation and were available to help make Atlanta a pilot city. "We have come," they said, "to offer Campus Crusade's nearly quarter of a century experience in training people in personal evangelism and discipleship to the local churches."

Dr. Stanley later recalled, "I knew it was God's answer to my own concern."

It was an evidence of how crucial it is for Christians to listen when God is imparting His vision to them. For God sees the overall pattern and how each part fits into the other.

Dr. Stanley's vision and Cobby Ware's concern were part of the plan God had impressed upon the leadership of the Campus Crusade for Christ movement in 1968. We believed we should pray and work for the fulfillment of our Lord's Great Commission in the United States by 1976 and the world by 1980. In response to our prayers for a spiritual awakening and revival in our nation, God gave us the vision of how to help reach our countrymen with the gospel, and we began to develop the strategy which was to become Here's Life, America.

One of the most important truths which I have learned during the more than 30 years of my exciting spiritual journey with Christ — and one that we claimed from the start of Here's Life, America — is the fact that when God tells us to do something He will give us the ability to do it well if only we will trust and obey Him: "It is God who works in you both to will and to do His good pleasure" (Philippians 2:13, KJV).

Thus, it was our responsibility to be obedient to the vision which He had given; it was His responsibility to work the necessary miracles that would result in fulfilling the vision which He had given.

We were confident that He would be faithful to give us the ability to help accomplish this seemingly impossible task. For, as the apostle Paul wrote to encourage us: "I can do everything God asks me to with the help of Christ who gives me the strength and power" (Philippians 4:13).

What happened in the United States by the end of 1976

and continues to happen in more than 200 cities through Here's Life, America and through many other men and movements leads us to the confident conclusion that if we are faithful to the vision God has given us, the second part of that vision — helping to spread the gospel throughout the entire world by the end of 1980 — will also become a reality!

God Gives Us Guidelines

During the formulative months of prayer and planning among our leadership, eight principles emerged that seemed to provide the foundation for a plan which could actually help us achieve the objectives of the Great Commission.

First, we recognized that if we were talking about affecting our entire nation, we must go where the people are — in cities. More than 75% of our population of 215 million people reside in just 265 metropolitan areas. Therefore, we needed a plan which would have one major objective — reaching the metropolitan communities of our nation, and from these major centers moving out to the 18,000 smaller communities of the country.

Second, we recognized that the resources for accomplishing this task *already resided* in local churches. Thousands of Christians are sitting in churches right now — ready for action.

Third, we determined that local leaders were needed in each metropolitan area — pastors and laymen who would be willing to commit their time and resources toward accomplishing the task. How many were needed? It is never as much a matter of quantity as of quality. Every great movement has started with only a small number of truly committed men. Lenin took Russia, a land of more than 100 million people at that time, beginning with just 17 men. Mao captured the most populous nation in the world through the total commitment of only a handful of "renegades." Hitler rose to power with the aid of his small band of "hoodlums" and "social outcasts." More positively, how many men did our Lord use to launch His worldwide enterprise? Only 12!

Fourth, we realized that Christians must pray and believe God for a plan to reach their cities for Christ.

Training for Warfare

Fifth, we anticipated that Christians would need to be trained in order to release their full potential. We are indeed involved in warfare — spiritual warfare. What commander would think of preparing for battle without training and equipping his troops to do what they are expected to do? In the same way, Christians must learn how to draw upon the power of the Holy Spirit in their lives *before* they can be effective witnesses (Acts 1:8). Christians must also be trained in disciple-making — winning others to Christ and then helping them grow in Christ to win still others and build them in the faith.

Sixth, we determined that at some point we needed to get the attention of an entire city. That can be done only through mass media — television, radio, newspapers, billboards, bumper stickers, etc.

Seventh, we reasoned that the city must be broken down into small, bite-size pieces so that each trained Christian could have his personal part in reaching the entire city for Christ. To do this a city would be divided into regions and neighborhoods, and ultimately to street blocks of approximately 50 homes each.

Eighth, we felt that churches should be assisted in developing ongoing discipleship and evangelism programs with their own congregations. They could then maintain a continual and stable impact for Christ in neighborhoods all around the city.

These eight principles were received in answer to much prayer and planning by our leadership. They became the acknowledged guidelines from God upon which the entire Here's Life, America movement would be based. Convinced that these principles were sound, we proceeded with the development of a detailed strategy.

Next came the step of faith to apply the plan in three different real life situations — Atlanta, Dallas and Nashville.

"Over and over again," marveled Bruce Cook, who

was later to become the national director of Here's Life, America, "I saw each of our eight principles accomplished — and often in miraculous ways. That way only God received the glory, and we were forced to live by faith — trusting God to accomplish what He said He would do."

As Bruce continued to assist the people of Atlanta in preparing for what was then called "*Agape* Atlanta," the movement was also gathering momentum in Dallas and Nashville. During the following year, lessons which began to point toward a workable "city saturation" strategy were learned in each city.

From Bob George, the Dallas coordinator, and his work at the First Baptist Church, emerged the concept of neighborhood church outreach groups — applying various evangelistic strategies in neighborhoods in the Dallas area.

From Sid Bruce, the Nashville coordinator, and Tom Cummings, a Nashville businessman and chairman of the executive committee, came the idea of using a computer to divide the city into workable units and to monitor the progress of calling on every household.

But it was in Atlanta that Bruce Cook, working with a dedicated team of concerned pastors and laymen, first had an opportunity to bring all the pieces of the plan together and to see a city begin to be saturated with the gospel message. Every step of the way was marked by a pattern of prayer, plans, work, problems, more prayer — resulting in miracles!

Putting the Plan into Action

In the beginning, as today, we in Campus Crusade felt that our role should have a low profile. We should do what we do best — assist, train and serve in a resource capacity. Thus, the plan called for organizing a local committee of pastors and laymen who, together with a trained Campus Crusade staff member, would provide the leadership for the effort. They would also be responsible for forming a special prayer emphasis, usually a 24-hour prayer chain.

Here's Life, America swung into high gear during May 1975 as thousands of Atlanta Christians prayed and worked together in an unprecedented effort to reach every household in the city with the message of God's love and forgiveness.

"It was as well organized as a presidential campaign," a TV reporter said, "but America has never seen anything like this!"

Indeed, the Here's Life, America movement did begin as a well-organized campaign. And it continued to gather momentum from the time it began in Atlanta, trumpeting a message on TV and radio, on billboards, in newspaper ads, on bumper stickers and lapel pins.

The message: "I found it! — new life in Christ!"

We are convinced that the strong emphasis on prayer played an important part in the success of the movement.

How It Worked

People were being reached with the good news of Jesus Christ in every conceivable way. Through the mass media — TV, radio, newspapers — and other means, the city was saturated with the phrase, "I found it!" People were encouraged to call in for a free booklet telling how they, too, could find new life in Christ. Through systematic neighborhood campaigns, workers went door-to-door, block-by-block, sharing the new life available in the person of Jesus Christ. They witnessed in every situation — at the market and the gas station, with a neighbor or fellow worker, on the bus, at school and over the phone.

Those who called the central telephone center as a result of seeing the "I found it!" phone number in ads were visited by trained block workers who introduced many to Jesus Christ. Many of these workers continue to experience the joy of seeing the new Christians grow in their faith through participation in follow-up Bible studies in their churches and homes.

An enthusiastic young woman commented, "People were going door-to-door, house-to-house, sharing their newfound faith with their friends and neighbors. And when that starts, you just don't shut it off."

Sharing Christ as a Way of Life

From the beginning of Here's Life in Atlanta, from one

end of the city to the other, people who had received training in evangelism and disciple-building in their local churches were doing their part in helping to fulfill the Great Commission in their city.

"During the initial weeks of Here's Life in Atlanta," Bruce Cook explained, "more than 140,000 households were contacted, and 25,000 phone calls were received from interested people, with more than 10,000 indicated decisions for Jesus Christ. That was just the beginning of a week-by-week continuous effort by church members to reach their city for Christ."

Testimonies were being shared of newfound joy and forgiveness through belief in Christ. Lives were being changed, families reunited. Christians were sharing the thrill of seeing their first converts won to Christ. Churches were experiencing new life and new growth. Atlanta was aflame with the power of God's love.

Claude Brown, one of Atlanta's leading citizens and owner of one of America's largest truck lines, said, "A year after the media campaign the Spirit of God still hovers over this city in a unique way as a result of the *Agape* Atlanta pilot project for the Here's Life, America movement."

Many of the thousands of people in Atlanta who went through training continue to share the good news of Jesus Christ as a way of life.

Pastor Charles Stanley looked back at what *Agape* Atlanta meant to pastors: "Not only have a lot of people found Christ but a lot of us pastors have found what we're looking for as a means of doing what we know ought to be done."

The key to the success of *Agape* Atlanta was the involvement of the 91 participating churches. Without the ongoing movement of evangelism and discipleship in these churches, the mass media campaign would not have been so effective because there would not have been workers to follow up the people who wanted to know more about Christ.

How can we describe what happened in Atlanta? Only in *miraculous* terms. As Nehemiah said in the Old Testament, when the Jerusalem wall was rebuilt in 52 days, "They realized that the work had been done with the help of our God" (Nehemiah 6:16).

What had begun as a vision from God — to reach the people of Atlanta with the good news of Jesus Christ — now, through prayer and the attendant miracles of God, was becoming a reality. It surely had been done with the help of our God. To Him be all glory and praise!

To those of us at Campus Crusade for Christ, the success of *Agape* Atlanta was confirmation from God that we were to go ahead with plans for helping to reach every city in our nation with the gospel. And so, in a short time, we were able to say to all of our fellow countrymen, "Here's Life, America!"

5
Moving on Faith

By the fall of 1976, it had become apparent that an unprecedented spiritual awakening was sweeping our nation. Here's Life, America, moving ahead on faith, was beginning to spread from city to city from our pilot campaigns in Atlanta, Dallas and Nashville. Within 12 months more than 200 metropolitan areas were being saturated with the claims of Christ through the mass media and telephone and personal contacts of thousands of trained workers.

The Blessing of Leadership

From the very beginning of the Here's Life movement God blessed the effort with effective faithful leadership. The Lord had used Bruce Cook in such a remarkable way in spearheading the leadership of the pilot city of Atlanta that I asked him to become the director for Here's Life, America campaigns across the United States. And I asked Paul Eshleman, who was the United States Field Director of Campus Crusade, to be co-director of Here's Life, America, involving staff members of Campus Crusade's various ministries — campus, lay, high school, military, prison and special ministries.

In addition, I looked to Steve Douglass, Campus Crusade's vice president for administration and director of the headquarters ministry, for his good counsel and assistance in this remarkable thrust of the Spirit.

Under the direction of Paul Eshleman, our field staff of Pat Means, John Lynch, Glenn Plate, Dave Sunde, Roger Randall and Roger Vann supplied leadership and coordination in the cities which participated in the movement. They, together with hundreds of other Campus Crusade staff members, recruited city leadership among Christian businessmen and established ongoing working relationships with the pastors of thousands of local churches.

The Here's Life, America leadership team, under the direction of Bruce Cook, played a major role in coordinating and directing the overall United States strategy. Bob Stark was overseer of the administrative activities of the movement. Regional coordinators were Pat MacMillan (West), Jim Heiskell (Southeast), Roy Box (Central), Ralph Walls (Northeast) and Ron Blue (Midwest).

A Price Worth Paying

The two-year period of Here's Life, America — 1975 through 1976, with a few cities going with their campaigns in 1977 — marked a high point in my personal walk of faith. I was living out of a suitcase most of the time, but fortunately, since I spent only a few days each month at Arrowhead Springs, my wife, Vonette, was often able to travel and minister with me. Our sons are both in college, so we were able to give Here's Life, America top priority.

Motivated by faith and guided by our Lord's Great Commission, the urgency continued to burn in my heart that America must be turned back to God. My concern was not only for America, but for the world. For America possesses the vast resources of money, manpower and technology that can help reach the rest of the world for Christ. I felt then as I do now that if we fail — if America is not reached for Christ — there is little hope for the rest of the world. So whatever the cost in personal sacrifice, it is a price that is well worth paying. Thus, with a life and death sense of urgency, I met day after day in city after city with pastors, city fathers, lay people and others, praying, planning and asking God to work His miracles. I did this joyfully with the assurance of His promise: "All authority in heaven and earth is given to Me" and "I will go with you" (Matthew 28:18,19).

A Growing Movement

Pastors and church leaders from a wide variety of denominations, together with business and professional men and women — in obedience to our Lord's commands — were stepping out on faith and taking significant amounts of time to lead the Here's Life movement in their cities.

Dr. Ralph Walls, a dentist in Indianapolis, upon hearing about Here's Life, America, moved on faith. He said, "This is what is needed in our city. I'll take off nine months from my practice to provide the leadership."

Dr. Bert Harned and his wife, Jan, have made a major impact for Christ in the state of Kansas and especially Kansas City during the last 20 years as associate staff for Campus Crusade. It was under their leadership that Campus Crusade actually began in the state of Kansas.

Eddie Burford, a Fort Worth businessman, was not only involved in launching the movement in his city, but, as a matter of faith, went on to commit 90% of his time to helping start Here's Life, America movements in other cities in Texas. Dr. Bill Buck, an orthodontist from Birmingham, Alabama, did the same. And there were others — Jerry Martin of St. Louis; Gene Quist from Minneapolis; Bill Fagan, New Orleans; Jim Sytora, Baton Rouge; Ron Harris, Denver; Jim Baker, West Palm Beach, Florida; Leroy Eger, Jacksonville, Florida; Dick Burr, Miami, Florida (also coordinator of Greater New York); Clarence Brenneman, Oakland; Dr. Henry Richter, Los Angeles; Don Shriver, Houston; Don Preston, Greenville, South Carolina; Gene Beekman, Oklahoma City; Hal Jones, Honolulu; Stan Oaks, Ft. Worth; C. Payne, Allentown, Pennsylvania; Phil Price, Omaha, Nebraska; Wick Waltmire, Fresno; Chuck Wheeler, Porter County, Indiana; Bob Thompson, Lincoln, Nebraska; Earl Stenehjem, Anchorage, Alaska. These men are but a representative sampling of the many who provided leadership roles as city coordinators.

Sharing a New Life

By faith, these men and thousands more men and women trusted God to open the doors for evangelism and discipleship in their cities. Among other things, they expected and saw miracles of God through four-week media campaigns. During the first week of these campaigns the "I found it!" slogan appeared throughout the cities, adorning billboards and bumper stickers, in newspaper ads, radio and TV spots and even on lapel pins. Because of faith, God opened unusual and unprecedented doors of opportunity in the mass media and further provided all the necessary funds.

As city residents started wondering exactly what had been found, the "reveal" portion of the campaign began. The media advertisements added to the original "I found it!" message, "You can find it too: new life in Jesus Christ," followed by a phone number to call for more information.

Names of those who called the campaign's "I found it!" center were referred to workers trained in communicating their faith in Christ. Workers phoned the callers from neighborhood phone centers, often located in the local churches, to arrange a time for them to bring a "Here's How You Can Find It Too" booklet to the caller's home. The trained worker then used this booklet, which contains the four Spiritual Laws with its simple gospel presentation, to explain the claims of Christ to the caller.

An innovation in the strategy following the Atlanta campaign was the neighborhood telephone center. It was used in this way: In addition to visiting the people who called in response to the "I found it!" ads, the workers were also responsible for contacting a block of homes in their area. They called each home from the neighborhood telephone center and explained the gospel.

"The most exciting place has been the neighborhood telephone center," says the Rev. Bob Radtke of Fresno's Bethany Mennonite Brethren Church.

Faithful workers assembled in these neighborhood telephone centers so that they could offer each other moral support and encouragement during the evening's phoning.

Mounting Enthusiasm

Lyle Richards, a layman from Calgary, one of the

Bruce Cook, National Director, Here's Life, America, addresses key leaders in a Here's Life city.

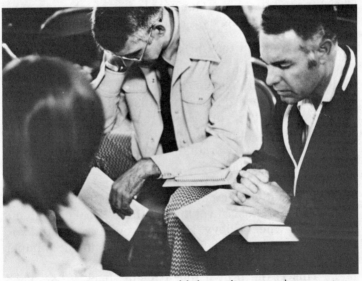

Billboards and TV spots would have been useless ventures without the most vital activity of all — prayer.

largest cities in western Canada, headed up the neighborhood phone center for his church.

"Some of the people coming to the phone center had been Christians for years," Lyle said. "And their eyes just sparkled with joy when they introduced someone to Christ over the phone.

"On the way down to the phone center, one man told us he didn't believe this would work," Lyle said. "He walked into the center and out of the first 10 people he called, seven received Christ."

Church members from Welch Avenue Baptist Church in Columbus, Ohio, according to the Rev. Paul Thompson, introduced more than 700 people to Christ during the campaign in that city. He said the church immediately started five-week Bible studies for new Christians and that these were an integral part of Here's Life. Additional studies were held in homes for those who could not attend the ones at the church.

"There's a new excitement in our church now," says Rev. Thompson. "At least half of our 250 trained members, including some of our very timid people, led someone to Christ for the first time. Our people feel much more comfortable in witnessing as a result of the campaign."

Millions Contacted for Christ

Literally millions of people's lives have been touched by the gospel through the initial phases of Here's Life, America. Some heard it as they called a local "I found it!" telephone number, others through the neighborhood phone centers, others through random contacts with trained Here's Life workers, and still others through the hour-long TV specials.

Jack McCreary, chairman of the Here's Life, Austin (Texas) executive committee, shared this unusual story: "A CB radio enthusiast got the message, 'Breaker 19 to the brown four-wheel Chevy. Hey, good buddy, what did you find?' The speaker was referring to the 'I found it!' bumper sticker on the other car.

" 'This is the brown four-wheeler back to ya', good buddy. I found a new life in Jesus Christ. Would you like to hear about it?'

" 'Thanks for the offer, but I don't have time,' the first replied.

"Then a voice from a semi-truck and trailer broke in, 'Breaker 19 to the brown four-wheel Chevy, this is a Mack 18-wheeler. Hey, good buddy, I'd like to hear about it. What's your 20 (location)?'

"The two vehicles, traveling in opposite directions on the interstate, pinpointed their locations and arranged a meeting place. The driver of the brown Chevrolet with the 'I found it!' bumper sticker walked across the highway and led the truck driver to Christ. This man was one of more than 2,800 recorded decisions for Christ in the beginning phase of Here's Life, Austin."

Sharing Before Surgery

A pastor in Columbus, Ohio, reported that during the campaign his people led 74 individuals to Christ in one night at their neighborhood phone center. A total of 60,750 people were called from the neighborhood phone centers in Columbus during the campaign; 4,600 of those received Christ and 897 were enrolled in Bible studies.

As a result of the Columbus outreach, a small boy being rolled into surgery noticed the "I found it!" button a nurse was wearing and asked, "Did you find it?"

"Yes," she replied, "Have you found new life in Christ, too?"

"Yes, I called the telephone center last night and told them I was having surgery today, and I wouldn't be home to get the booklet. So the worker told me about Jesus, and I asked Him into my heart."

The nurse took off her button and pinned it on the little boy's gown before she rolled him into the operating room.

Philadelphia, a city of 4.8 million people, was considered part of the section of the country most hardened to the gospel. But the seemingly impossible did happen there as nearly 10,000 trained black, white, Puerto Rican and Chinese Christians from both the suburbs and the inner city worked together to reach Philadelphia for Christ.

These trained workers came from 420 churches representing 19 denominations.

As a result, more than 270,000 people were contacted by phone, and 35,000 heard the Four Spiritual Laws presentation of the gospel. Reports of the 10,000 workers indicated that nearly 19,700 received Christ and 3,400 were enrolled in a five-week follow-up Bible study sponsored by a local church.

One church that was mobilized for Here's Life was the New Testament Church of Christ, a year-old church with a membership of 30. The Rev. Nathaniel Winslow started by training 95% of his people for the campaign, and by the time the campaign was in full swing, 42 people — including some from outside his church — had been trained to reach individuals for Christ. By the end of the campaign, 130 people contacted by church members received Christ and 198 were enrolled in follow-up Bible studies.

Another church, Pilgrim Baptist, under the leadership of Pastor David Wick, installed 15 phone lines in its church building and called people in the neighborhood from 9 a.m. to 10 p.m., seven days a week. During one day of phoning, 77 people received Christ, with approximately 1,000 total decisions recorded.

Pastor Douglas Barnes of Wallace Street Presbyterian Church in Indianapolis, Indiana, said, "Over the last three weeks we've had the opportunity to share Christ with more people than we have in the past 20 years."

Trained workers from Pastor Barnes' church and the other 115 congregations cooperating in Here's Life, Indianapolis have communicated the gospel to some 15,000 people. More than 5,000 responded by receiving Christ.

Russell E. Barker visited a woman who had phoned the neighborhood center where he worked in Montgomery, Alabama. "I started sharing Christ with her, then soon her husband came in and joined the discussion. Just as the three of us were ready to begin praying, a daughter came into the room. Shortly afterward, a second daughter and her boyfriend joined us. Before long all five of them followed me in a prayer to God, asking Christ to come into their lives and take control. There wasn't a dry eye in the room!"

Mile-high Miracles

In the mile-high city of Denver, Colorado, more than 3,000 workers shared Christ with some 38,000 persons who phoned in as a result of the "I found it!" media campaign. Of these, more than 7,500 received Christ.

"We've had five suicidal people who have called in," reported Earl Pickard, local director of Campus Crusade for Christ and project coordinator for the city. "I talked to one of them for 15 minutes, and I could tell he was genuinely depressed. He said he was lonely and had no reason to live. I sent two young men out to talk to him, and he soon prayed and received Christ."

Farmers in a small community near Calgary, Alberta, Canada were in their busiest season, but still worked faithfully every night to reach their community with the gospel. During the first week of the campaign, they phoned 130 people, shared Christ with 51, of whom 24 received Christ.

One pastor who visited Calgary during the campaign said, "I've had a desire to reach our city with the gospel, but until I saw this plan, I didn't have a clue as to how to do it. It would be a sin against God if we didn't use the materials He has given us to reach people."

A young boy from Fresno, California, was interested in attending a Here's Life follow-up Bible study. When the neighborhood worker called with information on the Bible study, the boy wasn't home, but his mother was and wanted to attend with her son. The worker also spoke with the boy's father and grandmother. By the end of the conversation, the whole family became interested in attending the Bible study.

Thousands of similar, exciting reports could be made concerning what God is doing in the more than 200 cities that participated in the Here's Life, America movement.

The excitement and enthusiasm of pastors and church members continues to spread. What had happened in the original 200 cities in 1976 and early 1977 was just the beginning of a movement of faith that is now sweeping across America and to other lands, influencing the lives of millions of people through the power of Jesus Christ.

6
Shattering Faith Barriers

Christians from around the country have learned to believe God for big things because of Here's Life, America. And many faith barriers have been shattered in the process.

Some people could not believe that large numbers of pastors would come together and work toward the same goals and objectives. Yet, one of the most important aspects of the Here's Life, America movement has been the feeling of brotherhood and love that has developed between pastors and churches of all denominations. Many pastors tell me that if there had not been one single decision for Christ, what has happened in the removal of barriers between pastors, laymen, churches and denominations would, in itself, have been worth all the investment of time and money.

There were those who could not believe that so many people could be trained. Yet, more than 300,000 people underwent an extensive 14-hour training program in personal evangelism and discipleship. Afterward, these same trained people became the workers in telephone centers answering the calls of their neighbors who wanted to know how they could find it, too. And, they were the ones who also took the initiative and either phoned their neighbors or called on them at their homes to tell them the good news about Jesus Christ. They are also the ones who are now seeking to disciple hundreds of thousands of new Christians through Bible studies and other forms of follow-up.

But, perhaps the greatest skepticism arose among people who just could not believe that the finances for Here's Life, America could be raised. Yet, in city after city, Here's Life committees rejoiced as God provided, often miraculously, the necessary funds for their city's mass media campaign, office supplies, training materials and equipment. For example, Bill Kanaga, senior partner of Arthur Young international accounting firm and chairman of New York's executive committee, reported that his city needed a budget of about one million dollars — and God supplied it!

Yes, people began to believe God for big things. But we should not be suprised, for as the apostle Paul wrote, " . . . My God will meet all your needs according to His glorious riches in Christ Jesus" (Philippians 4:19, NIV).

City after city across the country saw these "faith barriers" dissolved as pastors and laymen moved out in faith to saturate their communities with the gospel.

From the East

"One of the highlights of the campaign was the unity of churches from different denominations," said Tim Calahan, a lawyer who worked with the movement in the Washington, D. C., area. "People from different racial groups and different economic levels were all working together."

Two high school students in the area, Pam and Scott Cox, decided to call the members of the school band in which they played as a part of the campaign. The first five band members Scott called indicated that they would like to receive Christ into their lives. Twelve of the 17 students Scott called and 18 of the 23 his sister called received Christ as their Savior and Lord. All 30 of the new believers began meeting with more mature Christians to learn how to grow as Christians. More than 9,000 people in the Washington, D. C., area made decisions to receive Christ during the initial weeks of the campaign.

In the Springfield, Massachusetts, area, I am told that twice as many people as had ever before been involved in any combined effort among churches worked in the campaign. "Four times as much money was raised as had ever before been raised for any kind of cooperative effort," said Joe Webb, city coordinator for the area. "We were able to train 518 people out of a Christian population of approximately 5,000. Fuller School of World Missions experts said we mobilized a higher percentage of the available manpower than had ever before been brought together."

A girls' gang in Brooklyn paid $300 to have a rival high school girl killed. Soon, the girl was accosted in a subway, cut up, and pushed onto the subway tracks. She managed to survive, however. Meanwhile, her mother had called the Here's Life telephone center for an "I found it!" booklet to be delivered. When the campaign worker came to visit, only the recuperating daughter was home. The worker shared the gospel as presented in the booklet, and the girl prayed and received Christ. At a later meeting, her mother received Christ, too. Today, both mother and daughter are in Bible classes at a local church and are living new lives in Christ.

"It has been exciting to see the handiwork of God in Here's Life, New York," said Dick Burr, executive director of the city's campaign. In the first three weeks of the campaign, the believers in his area saw our Lord raise up over 15,000 prayer warriors to participate in the 24-hour prayer chain; more than 14,700 Christians who were trained to participate in mass evangelism and discipleship; more than 800 participating churches — independents and denominational affiliates; more than 85,000 people respond to the "I found it!" advertising; more than 355,000 evangelistic calls from the telephone center; more than 23,-000 people pray and receive Jesus as their Lord and Savior and more than 75,000 "Here's How You Can Find It Too" booklets were distributed. Nearly 7,000 have enrolled in Bible studies. We believe that these statistics represent only a small percentage of what God has actually done and is doing through Here's Life, New York.

We rejoice that this dynamic movement is continuing

through the ongoing commitment and participation of believers in many local churches throughout the New York area.

One of the major reasons for the remarkable movement of God's Spirit through Here's Life, New York could well be an ingenious idea which the Lord gave to my wife, Vonette. She ordered several New York City telephone directories and distributed pages to more than 3,000 of our staff in the United States and many others throughout the world. Hundreds of pastors and laymen volunteered to pray with our staff daily for each person whose name was listed on the hundreds of pages.

Thus, daily for many months, our staff and others were praying for tens of thousands of people in the New York City area by name. Is it any wonder that this city was visited by God in a unique way during the Here's Life media campaign — and that the movement is continuing with great blessing and harvest?

A New England municipality, Danbury, Connecticut, had encouraging results. The 170 workers who participated in this community of approximately 40,000 people saw 552 indicate decisions to receive Christ. This average of more than three decisions per worker was one of the highest in the country.

Many people contacted did not have assurance of their salvation. Lacy Young, who worked in a telephone center in Waynesville, North Carolina, shared in a letter to me how two-thirds of the professing Christians she contacted did not have assurance. Using the Four Spiritual Laws, Lacy told them how they could know beyond doubt that if they received Jesus into their lives as Savior and Lord they would be forgiven of their sins and have eternal life. One of the young women who received assurance of her salvation has since been used of God to lead 12 boys and girls to a saving faith in Jesus Christ!

Many reports have come to us about workers deciding to make one more phone call before quitting for the evening, only to have the person called pray and receive Christ. Such was the case with Judy Davis in Cincinnati, Ohio. She made "one last call" and reached a man who was going through a divorce and thought he had nothing left to live for. After she shared with him for some time, he prayed and invited Christ into his heart. Faith was no longer a barrier to him.

To the West

Faith barriers were also shattered in the West. "One of the highlights was the cooperation of the churches," said Jim Burke, city coordinator in Portland, Oregon, where 230 churches cooperated during the campaign. "Many pastors and laymen commented about how so many churches were working together to reach the city."

A crisis occurred during the Portland campaign when 80% of the "I found it!" TV schedule was cancelled and TV station personnel made it clear that nothing would change their minds. The people in Portland and several other cities began to pray. Later that day, the man who had flatly refused to allow any broadcast time to be purchased said to hurry over so that they could figure out a new schedule for airing the spots.

Even the barriers imposed by busy schedules were overcome. Carole Woolery of Corvallis, Oregon, kept calling back an elderly man who was always too busy to talk. Finally, he took time to listen to her, then admitted that though he was an active church member he did not feel spiritually ready to die. "I shared the gospel as contained in the Four Spiritual Laws with him, and he accepted Christ into his life without reservation! His joy came over the telephone lines!" Carole wrote to me. "About one month later that man passed on to be with his Savior. I praised the Lord that He impressed me to pursue that contact."

Carl Osterberg, coordinator for southern California, reported, "In the greater Los Angeles area, 950 churches, including 35 Oriental, 67 Hispanic and 75 black churches, cooperated in the campaign. A total of 27,000 people received Christ as their Savior during the initial stage of the campaign. No doubt many thousands of decisions were never recorded, and thousands more have made decisions for Christ since."

More than 300,000 people learned how to share their faith, whether they were in over-the-phone situations in the telephone centers or in spur-of-the-moment circumstances.

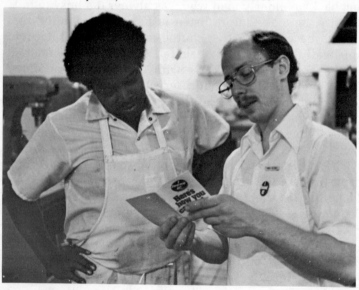

Two of the workers saw some unexpected results when they kept an appointment with a man. When they arrived, they found that he had been called to work, but his teenage son was at home, so they asked if they could talk with him. As they presented the gospel, the son asked Christ to take control of his life.

Then he asked the workers to wait while he called some of his friends to come to his home. They waited and five more boys arrived. Again the workers went through the Four Spiritual Laws and all five boys received Christ. One of the boys called his parents and they said, "We want to see what is happening over there. We'll be right over." When the boy's parents arrived, the two workers again shared the claims of Christ, and the parents prayed and invited Christ into their lives. The final outcome of that one follow-up appointment was 14 people praying and receiving Christ.

A Los Angeles pastor called one of the names on his telephone contact list, and the phone was slammed down after a violent reaction to his call. The next evening he inadvertently called the same number. "I told you, I've got too many problems of my own," said the man on the other end of the line. He was about to hang up again when the pastor asked if he could help with any of his problems. The man explained the unbearable guilt he had been carrying since his best friend had died in an accident in a race car that he had sold him. As the pastor told him how he could find peace, the man said he would like to commit his life to Christ.

At Oakland's Paradise Baptist Church, where Charles Johnson is pastor, 1,054 evangelistic phone calls were made by the members. As a result, more than 500 of those contacted prayed and received Christ and more than 100 of those enrolled in follow-up Bible studies.

Clarence Brenneman, city coordinator for Here's Life, Greater Bay Area, which included Oakland and San Francisco, reported on the results of the $300,000 three-week "I found it!" campaign: 10,000 trained workers from more than 325 participating churches made 260,000 evangelistic telephone calls and received another 40,000 calls in response to the media campaign. More than half of those who responded received copies of the booklet and more than 10,000 people were reported to have received Christ by the end of the three-week campaign. A daily prayer chain was formed with 15,000 people involved in interceding for the population in the Greater Bay area.

Clarence, an outstanding businessman from Eugene, Oregon, left his comfortable home and successful business to give more than a year of his time to help make the San Francisco-Oakland campaign an outstanding success. He and his wife, Vida, have been greatly used of God during the last 11 years as associate staff of Campus Crusade to help train tens of thousands of laymen and pastors.

Elsewhere in the West, some 5,800 people indicated decisions for Christ in the Phoenix area, according to the city coordinator, Tom Spencer. A crippled woman who was confined to a wheelchair took advantage of her CB radio during the campaign. As truck drivers came through town, she told them to come see her if they wanted to know what "I found it!" meant. Five truckers received Christ into their hearts through the witness of this woman.

In the Midwest

The same faith barriers that were shattered in the East and West also crumpled in the Midwest. "I resolved doubts about assurance of my salvation," said one Here's Life worker in the Chicago area. "And for the first time I shared my faith and that person received Christ." This worker's story was multiplied innumerable times across the country as thousands of trained workers received assurance of their salvation and thousands more led their first person to Christ. Our experience shows that as many as 20% of those who received Here's Life training received assurance of salvation as a result of the training and 70% of those trained had never before led anyone to the Lord.

"I believe our greatest strength has been our weakness," said Col. Nimrod McNair, chairman of the executive committee for the Chicago campaign. "Our media effort was weak because the major network stations refused to sell time for religious programming which was, unfortunately, true in most cities. Then, on November 19, the *Chicago Tribune* hit the streets with a negative story about Here's Life, Chicago on the second page. But God used the negative criticism to enable us to reach additional thousands with the gospel."

In the wake of the *Tribune* article came live interviews with NBC, ABC and CBS news and an article in Chicago's *Sun-Times*. As a result of the publicity from these sources, the awareness of Chicagoans about the campaign leaped from 20% of the population to almost 70%. "And we know that all that happens to us is working for our good if we love God and are fitting into His plans" (Romans 8:28).

The prayer ministry in each of the cities also played a key role in the success of the campaigns.

Christian radio station KTIS in the Minneapolis-St. Paul area made time available at 10 o'clock each morning during the campaign to pray for the needs of the day. "Many families shared that they united in prayer over breakfast during that time," said Doris Quist, prayer coordinator. Many of the churches have continued their prayer chains since the campaign ended.

A group of 28 European and 50 Canadian key pastors and laymen came to the Twin Cities to observe the campaign. "They became excited," said city coordinator Gene Quist, "and got a vision for launching Here's Life in their countries. It convinced us that what we were doing was something that could affect the rest of the world.

"An awakening in the churches is taking place because of Here's Life," Gene said. "A lot of pastors and laymen didn't believe it could happen. Now they are willing to believe God." More than 11,600 people said they invited Christ into their lives during the campaign with 552 signing up for the five-week follow-up Bible study for new Christians.

John Hall of St. Paul wrote: "Five received Jesus as Savior over the phone in response to my witness. I must add that in the beginning I was skeptical and didn't think it possible to introduce others to Christ and follow up personally by phone, but it does work."

Some people did not believe that the media campaign could be effective with students. But Ft. Hays State University in Ft. Hays, Kansas, was one of many campuses that saw successful media campaigns take place. Students at the college placed "I found it!" posters on their doors and elsewhere in the dormitories. More than 38% of the students who heard the claims of Christ responded by receiving Him into their lives.

The "I found it!" bumper sticker on Bob Kring's car in Plymouth, Michigan, brought so many inquiries over his CB radio that he became known among the local CBer's as the "Holy Roller."

Even the "I found it!" poster broke down faith barriers. Kathy Sellers of Lima, Ohio, wrote, "I had the 'I found it!' poster in my window. One afternoon a salesman came to my door and the first thing he said was, 'What did you find?' I told him and he said, 'That's neat. If Jesus is coming I don't want to miss Him.' So we went over the Four Spiritual Laws booklet, and he accepted Jesus before he left my home.

And the South

The stories of overcoming barriers to faith continue. "This was one of the greatest things in the world," said the Rev. Leroy Oesch of Lexington, Kentucky. "It welded our ministers together and got the word of Jesus Christ all over Lexington."

Roger Vann, Houston city coordinator, pointed to God's dealings with the media as an interesting development in their advertising. He reported, "Some of the major stations refused even to sell us time, but God changed their hearts, and they donated $20,000 of prime-time TV spots. It was better coverage than from both of the other stations for which we paid."

A Corpus Christi pastor, upon observing the difference that involvement in Here's Life had made in the life of one of his members, decided to take the training. As a result, he incorporated a clear presentation of the gospel into his Sunday message and for the first time in 25 years, gave an invitation for people to come forward if they wanted to receive Christ. To his amazement, approximately 250 people came forward. He remarked afterward that he needed to re-evaluate his entire ministry in light of this demonstration of people's hunger to know Christ personally.

When a Dothan, Alabama, man visited a high school student who had called the phone center, the boy was in his backyard playing basketball with four of his friends. The man joined in the game, and afterward the six of them gathered in a huddle as the man described his original reason for coming. Wondering what the huddle was all about, the first boy's mother and sister came out to see what was going on. All seven stated they would like to receive Christ.

This letter came to me from a woman in South Carolina: "My husband, who was a minister, and I had separated and divorce was not far away. I was in a state of great depression even while taking medication. I lost my job three times. I cried out to the Lord and felt that He hadn't heard me. As a result of my anguish my complexion worsened. So I went to see a dermatologist — Dr. Lynn Bradford, who was also a leader in the Here's Life campaign. He introduced me to Jesus Christ through the Four Spiritual Laws.

"I was impressed that a busy doctor would take time out to tell me about Jesus. I received Christ into my heart and became a Christian. The follow-up was educational and a gradual change in me resulted. Now I'm happier than I've ever been in my life. I eagerly look forward to God's plan for my life and for ways I can draw others to Christ."

Elsewhere in the South, a lady in a J.C. Penney's store in Augusta, Georgia, wore her "I found it!" button into a staff meeting of more than 200 employees. When she was asked by the chairman of the meeting what the button was all about, she responded by explaining the claims of Christ to the entire staff.

The Rev. Jack Turpin of North Miami Presbyterian Church was enthusiastic about the campaign's results in Miami. "We had never truly made an impact on this community until Here's Life came along," he said. "It seemed to be the Lord's timing so we trained 50 of our membership. What we have now is a nucleus of people who received Christ through the campaign and are potential disciplers."

One of the campaign workers from Turpin's church was walking down the aisle in a supermarket when a clerk who was stocking shelves asked, "What did you find?" She had spotted the "I found it!" bumper sticker on the shopper's car when she drove into the parking lot. The shopper told the clerk and offered to explain the gospel later. At the clerk's insistence, she began her presentation in the busy supermarket. In a few moments, the clerk invited Christ into her life. The worker started taking the clerk to church with her, and three weeks later this new believer joined the church.

"We placed a strong emphasis on follow-up," I was told by Dick Burr, city coordinator for Miami. As a result, 34% of those who invited Christ into their lives enrolled in follow-up Bible studies. This total of 2,240 people signing up for the Bible studies was one of the highest in the country.

Follow-up is a key part of Here's Life, America. I like the way Bruce Cook, national Here's Life, America director, recently described it: "I think what we're going to find is that Here's Life, America Phase I is the booster rocket to get the payload free of the atmosphere of lethargy. When trained Christians discover that God can use them to introduce others to Christ, they will want to become involved in helping these new Christians become disciples."

Further follow-up to Here's Life, America is the objective of Phase II of the strategy, which began in April of 1977. It is designed to train lay leaders to help the local churches sustain the evangelism and discipleship emphasis that was begun during the Phase I of Here's Life campaigns.

7
Claiming Our Nation Through Prayer

When Earl Pickard of the Campus Crusade staff was challenged in 1975 to develop a Here's Life, Denver campaign in the spring of 1976, his first reaction was that it could never happen in that city. But he spent three days in prayer and fasting, asking God to give him compassion and a burning desire to see all of Denver evangelized. He and his newly formed staff team began to claim the city by faith, and one night they went to the top of a hill overlooking Denver to pray.

Earl recalled that time: "As I prayed and meditated on the last few verses of Matthew nine, it hit me that Jesus was moved with compassion when He saw the people running around like sheep without a shepherd. I began to see that this described most of the people in Denver — that they were groping for answers.

"From here," Earl continued, "it was a matter of moving by faith; we believed God that He was going to reach Denver. We felt that if anything was going to happen in Denver it had to begin with prayer. As we shared our concern for a spiritual revival of God's people, we saw God begin to move supernaturally among His people in the city."

Eight months before the "I found it!" media campaign was started, 67 churches organized Here's Life prayer chains in which each church prayed one day a month for

10 to 12 hours. Answers to prayer included a larger number of involved churches, donations (which exceeded the cost of the campaign) and thousands whose lives were transformed by Christ.

The ministry of Campus Crusade in the state of Colorado actually began more than 20 years ago through the encouragement and financial investment of Carl Hoch and his wife, Margaret. They continue in their retired years to undergird Campus Crusade and the entire ministry through their prayers and financial investment.

What God did in Denver, He did in scores of other cities as well. It is because God has responded to the prayers of thousands of Christians who claimed the promise of II Chronicles 7:14 that Here's Life, America has been and continues to be so effective and fruitful. Time and time again, as requests were taken before God in prayer, He responded — in many cases, in truly miraculous ways. Here are but a few examples:

Praying for Telephones

Here's Life, Austin (Texas) was faced with a decision to either trust God that the local telephone company would complete its transition to new telephone equipment in time for the "I found it!" campaign, or, at great expense and inconvenience, move the telephone center away from the Here's Life "nerve center" to another part of town.

"The phone company said they planned to have our new lines installed one week before the campaign began," recalled city coordinator Alan Nagel, "so we decided to trust God that it would happen."

Delays developed, however, and it appeared that the new phone lines would not be installed in time after all. So, one night, about two weeks before the start of the campaign, at a Here's Life orientation meeting for workers, Alan brought up the phone situation as a prayer request.

During a break, George Pyland introduced himself to Alan, explaining that since he was in charge of all operations for the telephone company in central Texas, he might be able to help. He told Alan that he would look into the matter and report back as soon as possible.

As it turned out, one week before the campaign began, the new phone lines were put into operation at the telephone center.

"God had placed George in that meeting just to let us know that we shouldn't rely on ourselves," said Alan, "but rather start Here's Life and see it through, trusting God completely for all things and fully expecting Him to intervene in supernatural ways."

But prayer was nothing new to Alan and the Here's Life team in Austin, because the Great Commission Prayer Crusade (a Campus Crusade ministry which will be discussed later in this chapter) had been in operation in the area for two years prior to the start of Here's Life, America. Under the leadership of Frances Bradley, Pat Dahlrymple and Betty Turner, the prayer groups have seen many dramatic answers to prayer.

Betty Turner is the present chairman of the Austin Great Commission Prayer Crusade and Barbara Brockman was chairman of the Here's Life prayer chain. More than 1,000 people were praying around the clock for God to bless the efforts of the Here's Life movement in Austin.

Because of prayer and faith on the part of Austin's prayer warriors, God did bless their outreach. It began with church involvement. Historically, no more than 15 churches had ever participated together in evangelism in the city, but for Here's Life, America, some 67 churches, representing 14 denominations, came together to reach their city with the gospel of Jesus Christ. A local network affiliate TV station gave Here's Life a free spot announcement for each one purchased and greatly reduced the price for airing the "I found it!" TV special — all in answer to prayer!

Some 41,766 households in the Austin area were contacted by phone and nearly 5,000 calls came in as the result of the "I found it!" media campaign. There were opportunities to share Christ with almost 10,000 people — 2,508 of whom prayed over the phone and received Christ. Personal evangelism is continuing to this day, and more and more souls are being won into the kingdom. This all happened because God's children, out of obedience, came to Him in prayer and relied on Him to show them the way and to prepare the hearts of many who were in such need of the Savior.

Birth of the Prayer Movement

For more than 26 years prayer has been a major emphasis in my life and in the ministry of Campus Crusade for Christ. There have been thousands of answers to prayer, many of them dramatic demonstrations of God's power. Thus it was apparent to us that if this nationwide movement were to succeed, prayer must be an integral and vital part. God raised up Joyce Hopping to head up the prayer effort for Atlanta. Within one month, more than 1,-000 people had committed themselves to a 24-hour prayer chain to undergird the movement in Atlanta. One of those women was Rosalynn Carter, wife of President Jimmy Carter (who was then Georgia's Governor).

Among Mrs. Carter's contributions to Here's Life was a prayer meeting she held for 500 people in the Governor's Executive Mansion. Together, Governor and Mrs. Carter also helped to launch *Agape* Atlanta's media campaign by hosting a kick-off press conference.

I am convinced that it is because of prayer that Here's Life, America is the ongoing movement it has become. Thrilling stories by the thousands have been told of how God has been faithful to His promise, "You have not because you ask not" (James 4:2) and "If you ask anything according to God's will, He will hear and answer you" (I John 5:14,15).

In Canton, Ohio, the *Canton Repository*, a large daily newspaper, went on strike just before the city's "I found it!" campaign was to be launched. Bob Stratton, coordinator for Here's Life, Stark County (which included the city of Canton), prayed with his staff, asking God for an alternative to having newspaper advertising for the campaign.

"Then the Holy Spirit impressed on my heart a plan to replace our newspaper ads," Bob told us, "and the thought occurred to me to resort to doorknob hangers."

For a relatively nominal cost thousands of doorknob hangers were printed in a matter of days for use throughout the major metropolitan areas of Stark County, Ohio. They were distributed to churches throughout the area, whose members went door-to-door hanging the "I found it!" announcements on doorknobs.

"Immediately we began to hear the phones ring and could actually trace the responses on a map, following workers down the streets. The result was that doorknob hangers became a major medium for the 'I found it!' message in Canton, and more than half of our responses came as a result of them," Bob reported. "A total of 2,337 people prayed and received Christ as their personal Savior during the first three weeks of the campaign," he added.

Miracles in Minneapolis

Doris Quist, wife of the Here's Life coordinator for Minneapolis, was called of God to head up the prayer chain for her city's campaign.

"We set out by praying for God to raise up 24 churches whose members would form the 24-hour prayer chain for Here's Life, Twin Cities," Doris recalled. "But God had other plans! Instead of only 24 churches, He brought into the movement 235 churches — out of which 7,108 people committed themselves to be part of the Here's Life prayer chain.

"We saw thousands of answers to prayer," Doris said, "but perhaps the most dramatic answer came on the first Saturday afternoon of the start of the 'I found it!' campaign. Suddenly, all the telephones in the telephone center went dead — completely dead! So, we immediately prayed. At the conclusion of prayer, the problem had been solved in an unusual way, and the calls began coming in! Because of prayer, the telephones had been out for only about 15 minutes!"

Sensing the urgent need to continue reaching the people of Minneapolis and St. Paul with the gospel, and therefore the need for prayer on a round-the-clock basis, the Twin Cities' prayer chain there, as in many other cities, is continuing in operation.

Prayer: A Priority Emphasis

History records no great movement of the Spirit of God that has not been preceded by a very strong prayer emphasis. If there is any singular thing that God has honored and blessed most about Here's Life, America, I am convinced that it would be prayer. From the very beginning, prayer has had a priority emphasis in all of our planning and activities.

And rightly so, because God is God and has chosen to communicate with individuals through prayer. Our Savior Himself — to whom all authority in heaven was given — while here on earth spent much time praying. Now seated at the right hand of God the Father in the place of authority in heaven, He gives Himself to prayer in our behalf as our intercessor. Since He is our example, we can rightly conclude that prayer is the highest calling that a Christian can have.

Here's Life, America is the product of countless thousands of united, specific prayers — prayers for concerned business leaders to accept positions of responsibility on executive committees, prayers for dedicated pastors to undertake leadership roles among the local churches, prayers for much needed personnel in other areas of service, prayers for finances, prayers for training thousands upon thousands of workers, prayers that the news media might be objective and fair, prayers that many souls would be won for Jesus Christ.

At Campus Crusade's international headquarters at Arrowhead Springs, California, the staff of all our various ministries and outreaches prayed daily, under the leadership and organization of Paul Utley, Stottler Starr and Dan Erickson, for every geographical section of the nation, that the Here's Life movement would be used of God in bringing many souls into His kingdom.

Again and again, Bruce Cook, Paul Eshleman, Steve Douglass, Bob Stark and other leaders of the Here's Life movement met with me for prayer. We prayed in specific terms for God to direct us to key men and women for each major community of America to provide the leadership for Here's Life, to enlist the participation of thousands of churches, to facilitate the training of hundreds of thousands of workers, for effective use of the media for the "I found it!" campaigns and to assure the establishment of organization within the local churches for follow-up ministry and for millions of dollars to be raised in local communities to finance Here's Life, America in their areas.

In human terms it was very audacious of us to pray that Here's Life, America would be launched in each of the 265 major metropolitan areas above the 50,000 population level, and that from these major cities, the influence of the Here's Life "I found it!" media campaign would reach out to 18,000 smaller towns, villages and hamlets of America. But we were not operating on human terms; rather, we depended upon the supernatural power of God. So, as we prayed in faith, we began to see God work miraculously.

Millions Entered the Kingdom

At one time, in the fall of 1976, there were 143 major cities holding media campaigns at the same time. I am sure that it would not be an exaggeration to say that on a single day hundreds of thousands — if not millions — of people received Christ as a direct result of hearing the gospel through these media campaigns and through the personal witness of trained workers.

For example, the hour-long TV special we produced and aired in the fall of 1976 contained very moving and convincing testimonies. In the course of the program I gave a message in which there were three opportunities to receive Christ. The program was viewed by at least 100 million people, with as many as four television showings in some cities. I am sure it would not be an exaggeration to say that through that TV special alone, millions of people opened their hearts' door to Christ and God worked in the hearts of millions in answer to specific believing prayers.

Here's Life Prayer Strategy

The Here's Life, America church prayer strategy was designed to provide an opportunity for the local church to develop a strong prayer base to undergird its outreach and ministry. The fourfold purpose of this strategy was to: (1)

establish an *ongoing* prayer ministry built around a church prayer fellowship and prayer chain; (2) *train* church members to be effective in prayer; (3) *challenge* individuals to develop strong *personal* prayer lives; and (4) give individuals a *vision* for praying for their church, their city, the nation and the world.

The prayer effort during the "I found it!" campaign provided an opportunity for churches to train their people in prayer through prayer workshops and to be involved in a city-wide 24-hour prayer chain.

This was the beginning of an ongoing prayer strategy that is further developed in Phase II of Here's Life, America. Called the Church Prayer Strategy, this ongoing program is designed to build on the experience from the "I found it!" campaign and to provide for additional training and involvement in prayer in the local church.

Basically, the Church Prayer Strategy offers three avenues of prayer involvement to the individual: (1) to provide for continuing training in prayer through the mediated Dynamics of Prayer Workshop; (2) to establish weekly prayer fellowship in the church which will provide further instruction and motivation for prayer through the use of a new series of 20-minute films; and (3) to provide an opportunity for an ongoing prayer chain within the local church.

National Prayer Congress

In October 1976, we who are involved in the leadership of Campus Crusade felt a strong sense of urgency to call the evangelical leadership of America together to pray that we would meet the conditions of II Chronicles 7:14, and that God would send an awakening to our nation.

Because of my own deep sense of urgency and confidence in the power of prayer, I personally called more than 30 nationally known Christian leaders, representing the broad denominational spectrum of the church, and asked these people to participate in a National Prayer Congress at Dallas, Texas. Those responding by participating were such outstanding Christian leaders as Dr. W.A. Criswell, pastor of the First Baptist Church in Dallas;

Cliff Barrows of the Billy Graham Evangelistic Association; Jimmy Owens, composer of "If My People"; Dr. Billy Graham (on tape); Dr. Howard Hendricks, Chairman of the Department of Christian Education, Dallas Theological Seminary; Dr. Edward V. Hill, pastor of the Mt. Zion Baptist Church, Los Angeles; Dr. Robert H. Bowman, President of the Far East Broadcasting Company; Dr. Harold Fickett, President of Barrington College, Rhode Island; the Rev. Rex Humbard, pastor of Cathedral of Tomorrow; the Rev. Willie Richardson, pastor of Christian Stronghold Baptist Church, Philadelphia.

Dr. Jack McAlister, President of World Literature Crusade; Dr. Paul E. Toms, pastor of Park Street Church, Boston; Bruce Cook, National Director of Here's Life, America; Dr. James Kennedy, senior minister, Coral Ridge Presbyterian Church, Fort Lauderdale, Florida; Dr. Clayton Bell, pastor of Highland Park Presbyterian Church, Dallas; Corrie ten Boom, author, lecturer; Dr. J. Edwin Orr, professor, Fuller Theological Seminary, Pasadena, California.

Paul Eshleman, National Field Director, Campus Crusade; Dr. Sam Coker, pastor, Grace United Methodist Church, Atlanta, Georgia; Dr. Harold J. Ockenga, President, Gordon-Conwell Theological Seminary; Dr. Charles Stanley, pastor, First Baptist Church, Atlanta; Dr. Louis H. Evans, Sr., author, lecturer; Dr. Frank M. Barker, Jr., pastor, Briarwood Presbyterian Church, Birmingham, Alabama; Dr. Lloyd Ogilvie, pastor, First Presbyterian Church, Hollywood, California; Dr. Ben Armstrong, Executive Secretary, National Religious Broadcasters; Dr. Billy Melvin, Executive Director, National Association of Evangelicals; Pat Boone, singer, author; Pat Robertson, President, Christian Broadcasting Network, Inc.; Charles Colson, author, lecturer; and my wife, Vonette Bright, Director of the Great Commission Prayer Crusade.

More than 2,000 people came from across the nation for this unprecedented three-day Prayer Congress. God met with us in a wonderful way! I believe that what happened in Dallas was used of God to make an impact on our nation — the extent of which only He knows — that will be felt for generations to come.

There is no record of such a prayer congress in history. This is sad to hear when one considers that tens of thousands of conferences, religious and secular, on every possible subject, are held regularly. No doubt we need more congresses on prayer if our world is to be changed.

Now, as a result of that national prayer congress in Dallas, you can help conduct prayer congresses in your local communities because all the messages were taped and filmed and are now available for special prayer programs to be sent to every church and Christian organization in America and throughout the English-speaking world. These filmed lectures will motivate men and women to continue to pray for revival — that God will awaken America and the world to its need for prayer and for our Savior, the Lord Jesus Christ.

Great Commission Prayer Crusade

As part of Campus Crusade's firm belief in prayer, we are asking God to raise up at least five million Christians around the world who will enlist in the Great Commission Prayer Crusade. This ministry began in late 1971 when my wife, Vonette, invited three other Christian women who shared a common concern for the spiritual and moral climate of our nation to join with her in calling women to prayer. They believed that prayer was the only way to turn people to the source of personal, national and worldwide renewal — the transforming power of God's love and forgiveness through Jesus Christ.

Participants in some of the early prayer meetings were Mrs. Fred Dienert, speaker for the Billy Graham Evangelistic Association; Mrs. Harold Lindsell, wife of the editor of *Christianity Today*; and the late Mrs. Howard Davison, of International Christian Leadership. Mrs. Billy Graham served as honorary chairman.

As a result of the enthusiastic encouragement of pastors and laymen around the world, the movement ceased to be one for women only and now includes men and students representing the entire body of Christ. Within the movement are prayer rallies and prayer groups in many cities. The monthly Praise and Prayer newsletter is mailed to thousands of individuals and groups who are supporting the cause of Christ around the world. There are manuals for strategy and instruction, along with other teaching materials to assist Christians in developing more effective prayer lives. Representatives travel far and wide, encouraging and training individuals and groups in developing effective prayer ministries.

The Great Commission Prayer Crusade is a servant to the local church, seeking to unite Christians of all denominations and organizations to pray for a moral and spiritual awakening throughout the world. This will be accomplished as individuals learn how to pray effectively, and as new prayer groups are formed and already existing ones are united and expanded.

Resources of God

As Christians, God has given us the most effective possible means for changing the lives of men and nations — that means is, of course, prayer. God has literally made available to us a vast reservoir of power, wisdom and grace beyond words to describe. All we must do is be willing to trust and obey Him.

God said to Jeremiah, "Call unto Me, and I will answer thee, and show thee great and mighty things, which thou knowest not" (Jeremiah 33:3, KJV).

Remember, the one who made that statement is the one who is the mighty risen Son of God in whom dwells all the fullness of the Godhead bodily; the one who has commissioned us to go into all the world and preach the gospel and make disciples of all nations; the one who said, "All authority has been given Me in heaven and on earth; . . . Lo, I am with you always" (Matthew 28:18, 20, KJV). He is the one who said, "If you ask Me anything in My name, I will do it" (John 14:14, KJV). Consider well these promises of God, for the mighty resources of deity are available to you if you are a child of God.

There is no higher calling available to man than the privilege of prayer. I encourage you to contact the Great Commission Prayer Crusade, Arrowhead Springs, San Bernardino, California 92414, for additional information on how you can have a part in helping to change the world through prayer. In the meantime, I would also encourage you to arrange to have the prayer seminar on "How to Pray" presented to the members of your church and the churches of your city, along with various other films from the October, 1976, National Prayer Congress.

8
God's Direction Through Finances

The financial policy for Here's Life, America requires that each city in the movement raise its own funds. However, as the movement spread to more and more cities in the beginning, it became apparent that many metropolitan areas were unable to raise the necessary funds to finance their "I found it!" campaigns. At that point I asked Jim McKinney, director of our development department, to be available with his staff to assist wherever needed.

Through Jim and his staff, God opened to us the opportunity to assist the local finance committees as financial consultants to most of the Here's Life city campaigns.

The Faithfulness of God

Since it is the command of our Lord Jesus to go into all the world and preach the gospel, we know that He will make it possible — if only we will trust and obey Him! God would never call us to a task only to forsake us. "Lo, I am with you always," Jesus promised, "even unto the end of the world" (Matthew 28:20, KJV). And the apostle Paul reminds us, "Faithful is He that calls you, who will also do it" (I Thessalonians 5:24, KJV).

Earl Pickard, coordinator for Here's Life, Denver, and his staff and workers constantly brought the financial needs of their city's campaign before the Lord. Consequently, because of the strong prayer emphasis, finances were never a real problem; funds steadily came in, day by day, in answer to prayer. This was true even when Here's Life, Denver needed to pay $12,000 for media advertising and $3,400 were still lacking — right up to the day the payment was due.

One staff member shared the need at a businessmen's Bible study and returned to the campaign office with $1,600. But they still needed $1,800. Later that afternoon a businessman whom Earl had previously challenged to invest in the outreach called to say he couldn't attend a meeting that afternoon, but asked where he could send a check for $2,000. Earl and the staff were filled with praise and thanksgiving to God for His faithfulness in answering their prayers and meeting their financial needs in the campaign.

God chose to use the subject of finances to introduce many to Christ. For example, Denver's financial coordinator, Lee Ashley, presented a fund development film presentation to a very dear friend of his — an 82-year-old widow. "Through this," Lee joyfully shared later, "she prayed with me and received Christ!"

Cliff Hardin, city coordinator for Kansas City, reported, "Here's Life had only $500 in the bank on the deadline date for an installment payment of $20,000 for the television budget, but the $19,500 needed came in that day in answer to prayers. People began phoning in with offers of money. The last $3,000 came in at the last minute — exactly 5 p.m. — while the staff were praying for a "miracle." God had demonstrated once again that He is faithful in meeting His children's needs.

Meeting Specific Needs

Dave Balch, coordinator for Here's Life, Columbus, Ohio, explained how God met their financial needs: "The Lord brought in just the amount of money we needed and not much more," he said. "After I wrote the check for $26,000 to pay for television time, we had $40 left. The same was true after we paid for the billboards. God kept us trusting Him — that's for sure!"

Dave continued, "People have given both big and

small financial gifts. One man advanced us $50,000 for initial expenses and another gave us a check for $4,500. Then a woman brought in an envelope with 92 one-dollar bills in it and a man gave us his tax refund check for $365. One man contributed $500 that he had borrowed. Another sold some stock for $500 and donated it. As we needed more money, God sent it in, always in answer to prayer."

In many cities we encountered policies at television stations that prevented Here's Life from purchasing air time for "I found it!" spots. But what appeared at first to be an obstacle turned out to be a financial blessing. In Raleigh, North Carolina, for example, a TV station had the policy of not selling air time for religious programming. But after the station's program director saw a presentation of some of the spots, he decided to donate $13,000 worth of air time to Here's Life — which made it possible to air the one-minute and 10-second spots as well as the hour-long "I found it!" TV special.

John Temple, city coordinator for Here's Life, Knoxville, Tennessee, shared how God provided his city's campaign with specific amounts of money, just as they were needed. The first time, $11,000 was needed. John called a meeting of prospective donors. "Only two of the three key individuals came," he recalled, "and after we presented our needs, one man said he would give $5,000 and underwrite another $5,000, and the second man said he would give $1,000."

On another occasion, a local attorney worked closely with John to set up a meeting with 13 couples at a country club. "God impressed me to pray for $20,000 to be raised at that meeting," John shared. "After the meeting and dinner, those 13 couples contributed over $21,000 to Here's Life, Knoxville!"

Direction Through Finances

Testimony after testimony has come to us from people involved in the Here's Life movement telling how God dealt with them through finances. John Gillis, chairman of the Spokane, Washington, sponsoring committee, was one such person.

"I believe that God's most amazing miracle in putting together our financial operation was first of all how He showed me after prayer and consideration that I could personally give an amount that was probably five to 10 times what I had thought was possible," he shared.

Organization had much to do with fund-raising in many of the cities, but God often saw fit to by-pass such approaches. The situation in the city of Tucson, Arizona, was a case in point. "We came into the Here's Life movement very late," explained Tucson's city coordinator Rufe Livingston. "We formed our committee sometime in the latter part of August and the Lord just kept raising up the proper person for the task at hand. As we look back and reflect, it had to be God's hand in the timing of things. In the raising of funds, for example, we never did get a fund-raising sponsor or chairman or committee, but the Lord just raised up the money in fantastic ways."

One such way was through the sacrificial giving of people whose hearts had been burdened for reaching their city with the gospel.

"We had one man," recalled Rufe, "who had been rehabilitated by the Salvation Army and was a truck driver for that organization. He gave us a gift of $1,000, and I know it was a sacrificial gift of love."

Such giving was not uncommon throughout the Here's Life campaign. Mature Christians, who had learned from experience to trust God in the area of giving, responded to the financial needs of their Here's Life campaigns.

Recognizing God's Priorities First

One man's heart had such a burning desire for reaching his region with the gospel that even a great personal loss could not deter him from doing what God was directing him to do.

Mallory Mays, executive committee chairman for Here's Life, Central Missouri, told us the story: "God raised our money and met our needs exactly when it was necessary. We trusted Him for it, and He caused us all to come in faith, believing that He was truly concerned in working with us for our campaign. The thing that was especially significant during the campaign was when one of the checks — for $1,300 — came from a man whose wife had been killed in an automobile accident that day. He had delivered that check to our Sedalia office a few hours after his wife had died, saying he wanted this money to go to Here's Life — wanted to see the movement become a reality in Central Missouri."

Sharing from God's Abundance

When Here's Life, Upper Piedmont, South Carolina, received from God more money than they needed they felt impressed to share it with another city. "Four of us got on our knees and turned our financial need of $65,300 over to the Lord," recalled Don Preston, city coordinator from Greenville. "Then we got up from our knees and went to the bank and signed a note as an act of faith and obedience. Then, that very same day, close to $10,000 came into our office. The end result was that we received about $78,000, and we felt impressed by God to use the surplus in sending a man to assist with the Greater New York campaign and to make a contribution of $12,000 to help reach the people of New York with the gospel.

"We praise God for what has happened," Don said enthusiastically. "We have really had a fantastic time, and our committee is still intact. We will be going right into Here's Life Phase II, I'm sure."

How God Uses Finances

Just as it happened in Greenville, so it has happened in scores of other cities around the country. God consistently used finances to strengthen the faith of those involved in the campaigns. Over and over again the thrust of the principles former Campus Crusade associate staff member Larry Burkett shares in his book *Christian Financial Concepts* (Campus Crusade for Christ) became apparent, Larry explains eight ways in which God can use finances to bless our lives:

Trust: God promises us that He will provide all our needs if we place our total trust in Him. Jesus said: "So don't worry at all about having enough food and clothing.

Your heavenly Father already knows perfectly well that you need them, and He will give them to you if you give Him first place in your life and live as He wants you to" (Matthew 6:32,33).

Ability to supply: As God's children, we can trust God to answer our prayers. Jesus promised: "If you abide in Me, and My words abide in you, ask what you will and it shall be done unto you" (John 15:7), and, "You can pray for anything, and if you believe, you have it; it's yours!" (Mark 11:24).

Trustworthiness: God expects certain standards from us in our handling of money and material possessions. Jesus said: "And if you are untrustworthy about worldly wealth, who will trust you with the true riches of heaven?" (Luke 16:11).

Love: Many Christians fail to trust God in financial matters because inwardly they believe God wants to deprive and punish them. Yet, the Bible shows how God demonstrates His love for His children: "And if you hardhearted, sinful men know how to give good gifts to your children, won't your Father in heaven even more certainly give good gifts to those who ask Him for them?" (Matthew 7:11).

Power: God wants to show us that He will do what He promises — that, as His children, Christians can share in His riches. "For the Scriptures tell us that no one who believes in Christ will ever be disappointed. Jew and Gentile are the same in this respect: they all have the same Lord who generously gives riches to all those who ask Him for them" (Romans 10:11,12).

Unification: God uses material possessions to unify the body of Christ. "Right now you have plenty and can help them; then at some other time they can share with you when you need it. In this way each will have as much as he needs. Do you remember what the Scriptures say about this? 'He that gathered much had nothing left over, and he that gathered little had enough.' So you also should share with those in need" (II Corinthians 8:14,15).

Direction: One of the most important characteristics of a Christian commitment is *patience*. It is virtually impossible to be obedient and impatient at the same time. God will use money as one of the tests of our obedience to His will rather than to our own. The wisdom of Proverbs reminds us: "In everything you do, put God first, and He will direct you and crown your efforts with success" (Proverbs 3:6).

So if we are patient and obedient to God with our finances, He will reward us. This promise is amplified in the apostle Paul's letter to the Galatian church: "And let us not get tired of doing what is right, for after awhile we will reap a harvest of blessing if we don't get discouraged and give up" (Galatians 6:9).

Witness: The use of money is one of the most effective witnesses to many non-Christians. It is one thing to say you love others, but do you show that love? God's Word instructs us to share from the abundance He has given us: "For the poor shall never cease out of the land: therefore I command thee, saying, Thou shalt open thine hand wide unto thy brother, to thy poor, and to thy needy, in thy land" (Deuteronomy 15:11, KJV).

In the Gospel of Matthew we are shown that those in need are of special concern to our Lord. Jesus said: "When you refused to help the least of these My brothers, you were refusing help to Me" (Matthew 25:45). Therefore, if we really love our Lord Jesus and desire to trust Him and be obedient to Him, then we will be extending financial and other practical help to those who have needs. And certainly there is no greater need among men today than to know Christ personally as Savior and Lord. No greater investment can be made than an investment that will result in a person receiving Christ and becoming a true disciple of our Lord.

I give praise and thanksgiving to God for the many Christians who have invested in the discipleship and evangelistic efforts of Here's Life, as well as in the overall ministry of Campus Crusade. Those investments have played an important role in individuals becoming a part of the kingdom of God. No man can set a value on the gift of eternal life. No dollar amount can be estimated. It is a priceless gift, and it is one, while from God, that we as

Christians have the privilege of offering to all who will receive it through confessing that Jesus Christ is Lord. That priceless gift was offered to millions upon millions of people through the Here's Life, America movement. We thank our Lord that so many more people can now say: "I found it! — new life in Christ!" because of the personal prayers and financial investments of so many faithful followers of our Lord Jesus Christ.

As one enthusiastic participant in Here's Life, America remarked, "The total financial cost of Here's Life, America in more than 200 metropolitan areas and thousands of smaller cities was more than $8 million — which is no small sum of money. Yet, the benefits that have already been tabulated — apart from even greater results that we will never know about — make it all worthwhile. Here's Life, America, in my opinion, is the best financial investment for the cause of Christ that I have ever heard of."

Another businessman observed, "A man would be a fool not to invest money in a movement like Here's Life, America. Where could you find a better investment for the Lord?"

Still another — who gave several thousand dollars to his city's Here's Life — said: "I consider this the greatest investment for our Lord that I ever made. And I would gladly do it again!"

9
Sharing New Life on TV

Upon release from the hospital following recovery time from a suicide attempt, a Bellingham, Washington, college professor was overcome by depression once again and phoned the hospital's chaplain out of desperation. Since the chaplain also served as prayer chairman for Here's Life, Bellingham, he advised the professor to watch the "I found it!" television special which was on at that very moment.

The professor turned on his TV set to hear Dean Jones, Charles Colson and other individuals share how they had found a new life in Jesus Christ. Twenty minutes later, the professor phoned the chaplain again, exclaiming, "I did it! I found it!" Today that professor is growing in his faith, attending church regularly, and witnessing to his family — and he's no longer burdened by chronic depression.

Deluged with Calls

Telephone centers around the country report that they were deluged with calls during the time periods the two Here's Life TV specials were being aired. In Denver, for example, more than 2,000 calls came in over only 40 phones. In the various cities, in an attempt to keep the lines open for the callers, we established the policy of taking the caller's name and phone number, then calling him back at a later time when in-coming calls dropped back to normal.

But a Knoxville, Tennessee, newspaper editor was so moved by the TV special that he could not wait until the program was over for his call to be returned. So, he eagerly sought to locate his sister who happened to be on staff with Campus Crusade in another part of the country. After many calls he finally located her at a meeting she was attending and told her he wanted to find a new life in Jesus Christ — now! She shared the Four Spiritual Laws with her brother over the phone, then prayed with him. Later, when a Here's Life worker returned his phone call, the editor excitedly told him, "I've just received Christ! I'm a new believer!"

While the TV specials continue to be shown around the country, and as new Here's Life campaigns are launched in more and more cities, our consulting media specialists estimate that more than 175 million people in America ultimately will have the opportunity to see them and hear how they can find a new life in Christ. On each program a local phone number is given to enable viewers to call in to the telephone center in their city and ask to have a "Here's How You Can Find It, Too!" booklet delivered to their home.

The booklet contains several testimonies, some of which were shared on TV by the people who experienced them, as well as the Four Spiritual Laws.

"I Found It!" TV Special

Dean Jones, popular star of motion pictures and stage, was my co-host for our first "I Found It!" TV special. The 60-minute program presented some of the most candid, intimate moments you will ever likely see on television. My guests shared their very personal stories. They talked about their hopes, their fears, their joys, their struggles. They talked about life as it is for each of us everyday. And all of them told about a discovery that caused them to say, "I found it!" — a discovery that dramatically changed their lives for the better when they received Christ.

Cameramen prepare to film Dean Jones, host of the "I found it!" television special.

Pearl Bailey sings to the nation's people on the "Here's Life, America" TV special.

Born Again

Charles Colson, author of the best-seller *Born Again*, shared on the program how he had looked to the power and influence of national politics to bring fame and security into his life. As you know, because of Watergate, it turned into disappointment and despair for him. But it did not end there, because he later found a new life in Christ!

"Through that dark summer of 1973," Chuck recalled, "when Watergate really engulfed the nation and the poison just flowed through the city of Washington, the emptiness of my life continued. I thought I was changing the world, and I thought I was building power and prestige for myself, but I saw so much of it crumbling away."

But in that terribly dark, depressing time, Chuck was witnessed to by an old friend and business acquaintance — Tom Phillips.

"We spent a long evening," Chuck remembered. "He asked me to pray at the end of the evening. And it was overpowering. I didn't let on. I still was proud. I was the Washington lawyer, the presidential *confidante*."

When Chuck went out to his car afterward, he was crying so hard he could not get the key into the car's ignition, and this was the fellow who was known in the press as the toughest of the Nixon tough guys and the White House hatchet man.

"I sat that night a long time, alone," he told the TV audience. "But I now know, not alone at all. Probably for the first time in my life, not alone. Praying in a very bumbling way. I didn't know the right words, but I just knew that God was hearing me, and I just asked Him to take me."

A Star Is Born — Again!

Dean Jones has been called the most popular star at Walt Disney studio since Mickey Mouse. But that stardom did not bring happiness to Dean. Instead, it took a miracle of God.

"I found new life in Jesus," Dean told our TV audience. "I searched for many years for some fulfillment. There was a place somewhere within me that even stardom, a lot of money, or occasionally winning a motorcycle race could not fill."

While doing a play in Cherry Hill, New Jersey, Dean came to the point in his life of inviting Christ into his heart.

"I prayed off and on for three days something like, 'God, if You exist and You will make Yourself known to me in some way, give me some feeling of the reality of Your existence, I'll serve You the rest of my life.' Then it happened suddenly. I had peace. I had joy. I had tranquility. I was filled. I was empty no more!"

Dean then told the TV viewers: "So that's how today I can tell you that it's possible for you to find it, too — a new life in Jesus Christ. I know because it's happened to me. A miracle took place in my heart when I gave my life to Jesus."

Here's Life TV Tribute

Our second TV special, which was first broadcast in the spring of 1977, was a tribute to the hundreds of thousands of lay people and pastors from more than 14,000 churches of all denominations in more than 200 major cities across America who are a part of Here's Life, America. Living out of a suitcase for nearly two years, and speaking in a different city almost everyday, I have had the privilege of seeing the Here's Life, America movement at close range. So I felt led of God to share with millions of TV viewers what has been happening across the nation, so that they, too, would join with us in praising and serving our wonderful Lord.

In the program, Johnny Mann, Roy Rogers, Dale Evans and Pearl Bailey take us to a group of representative cities where Here's Life, America has been reaping an incredible spiritual harvest.

The program was produced for us by Dick Ross, who has done many motion pictures and major televison specials for the cause of Christ. Dick recalls the initial impact that Here's Life, America had on him when he started production of the program in the fall of 1976:

"We took the crew to Miami, Houston and Philadelphia to document the excitement and results of the mass media campaigns. I was totally unprepared for what I saw and sensed in those cities. For more than 21 years, I have been involved in recording on film the mighty works of our Lord. But never have I seen a local, church-oriented discipleship movement to compare with the Campus Crusade Here's Life concept. It was a thrilling sight!"

One of my co-hosts was Johnny Mann, whose blend of great musicianship and newfound love for Christ is a constant inspiration to all who know him.

"Here's Life, America was only an experimental idea two years ago, when something happened in my own life," Johnny shared with our TV audience. "To use the familiar Here's Life slogan, 'I found it! — new life in Jesus Christ.' Which means, I can now identify with many of the life-changing experiences you are about to see and hear in a kaleidoscope of personal witness from across the land."

And indeed, we heard and saw the tremendous spiritual impact Here's Life, America is having in cities across the nation.

Challenged Thousands

Edwin Pope, sports editor of the *Miami Herald*, told how Here's Life, South Florida, including the areas of Palm Beach, Fort Lauderdale and Miami, led by 250 churches and 7,800 trained Christian workers, challenged tens of thousands to personally consider the claims of Christ.

Our cameras recorded the testimonies of many people who had shared Christ and many who had received Him as Savior and Lord during the campaign. And so it was, in city after city across the nation.

At various times during our television odyssey across America, Johnny Mann and the Johnny Mann singers blessed us with such beautiful songs of praise as, "I Found It!," "That the World May Know" and "Because He Lives."

Among the many campaigns during the Thanksgiving season of 1976 was one in Houston, Texas. And in our TV studio, to give us a glimpse of Here's Life, Houston, was a couple whose personal witness and towering talents have made them two of the most beloved stars in show business,

Vonette and I met with Roy Rogers and Dale Evans on the set of "Here's Life, America."

Johnny Mann and the Johnny Mann Singers and Orchestra brought music into American homes on the television special.

and two of our dearest friends for more than 30 years, Roy Rogers and Dale Evans.

While Roy and Dale have known popularity and success, their lives have been struck time and again by tragedy and sorrow. Roy had adopted his first child, then he and his first wife had two children of their own; but only six days after their second child was born his wife died. About a year and a half later, Roy married Dale Evans, who had one son from a former marriage. Roy and Dale had one child — a borderline mongoloid, whom they later lost. After that, a son died while in military service and a daughter was killed in a bus collision.

"We had several tragedies," Roy told me in his dressing room between scenes, "and I just don't think we'd have been able to handle them like we did if we hadn't known Jesus. I think today the answer for the world's problems can only be solved by the love and power of Jesus Christ."

Dale had accepted Christ as her Savior when she was only 10 years old, but it wasn't until later years, thanks to the persistence of her son, that she let Christ become *Lord* of her life. "It was the greatest decision that I ever made in my whole life," she said, "because my life was just transformed, right then, when I really negotiated with God, and I asked Jesus to become personal to me, and vital to me, and make His presence known to me. And my life was changed, immediately. Everything that's happened to me that's of any note at all, any worth whatsoever, is a direct result of my commitment to Jesus Christ. Through Him I received a beautiful, new life. It's like my son said, 'Here's life — take it.' Here's Life, America is saying that today — to literally millions of people."

"The Chance to See God"

One of the most moving moments of our Here's Life, America TV tribute came when our guest Pearl Bailey sang the "Battle Hymn of the Republic." It was not a song she sang casually, for as she shared with us following video-taping that day, Jesus Christ has given her new life — and in a dramatic way. "I had the chance to see God perform miracles in my own life," she recalled, "in 1972, when I medically passed away. I know there are doctors, and I know they do great things, but I also know, that only the True Physician is the reason I'm inhaling and exhaling again. Every day I pick up my little Bible and read it, and I ask Him to give me more strength, to give me more courage."

In addition to blessing our TV viewers with her singing, Pearl hosted a film visit to Here's Life, Philadelphia — a city where her mother once lived.

"Mama's house in Philadelphia was never really large enough for all of us children. But someday we'll have a new one . . . the Main House, I mean. With God to watch over. Until then, like the whole human family, we sit and wait — in grief, in hurt, in remorse, in shame, in pity, but older, wiser, with more compassion, more understanding, more love. And the family will grow larger. And one day we'll all come home again. And the Landlord will live with us."

Pearl so eloquently reminds us that when all is said and done, it all comes down to the worth of the single soul, the individual.

You Are Important to God

In God's sight, you are important. You are why He sent His son. You are the reason Christ died — and rose again, that He might go to prepare those mansions Pearl spoke about.

There are four things that Jesus Christ wants to do for you . . . and only He can do them. First, He is the only one who can pardon you, forgive your sins. Second, He alone can give you purpose for life. Third, He alone can give you peace for a troubled heart. And finally, only He can give you power to live an abundant life.

Won't you pray right now, asking Him to do these things in your life, to be your Lord and Savior? If you do, you, too, will experience new life in Christ.

10
A Way of Life

Marjorie Dickens of Salem, Oregon, wrote to share that the training and experience she received in Here's Life has given her a new victory in Christ.

"I learned from the Way of Life training," she said, "to better appropriate the wonderful promises God gives us in His Word. I have a new assurance that I am walking in the fullness and control of the Holy Spirit. I led my first person to Christ! Now, with Christ's help, I have found a new, abundant life of witnessing and living for Him and in Him!"

A church music director wrote that the Way of Life training he received in Here's Life, America "was one of the factors that caused me to realize that the lack of 'real joy' in my life was because of the need of Christ on the throne of my life. I am now experiencing that joy more each day."

"I feel as though I am a more useful vessel for God," wrote Donna Poe of Buena Park, California, "because I took the time to learn how to effectively share my faith."

And a Here's Life worker in Denver concluded his testimony by jubilantly announcing, "I expect to lead people to Jesus as a way of life from now on!"

Key Ingredient

To Christians in thousands of local churches across our

great nation, reaching their neighborhoods for Jesus Christ is fast becoming a way of life. A key ingredient in Here's Life, America is, in fact, the Way of Life Plan. It is a strategy to assist the local church in developing a movement of evangelism and discipleship that will have a continuing impact in the community.

And that is the main thrust of Here's Life, America: building into the lives of the members of the local church a movement of evangelism and discipleship that will continue long after the mass media campaign has ended and until our Lord returns.

The plan is called the Way of Life Plan because it is designed to help believers experience a more abundant life in Jesus Christ and to share with others their faith in Him as a *way of life*. The plan itself was originated and developed because the staff of Campus Crusade believed that the local church is the key for reaching the neighborhoods of this country and the world for our Savior, and for building men and women into effective disciples. They believed this plan could help the churches reach their potential. Today, many churches are in the various stages of incorporating the Way of Life Plan into their training programs.

We call this process of building men and women into disciples "spiritual multiplication." It is based on a principle described by the apostle Paul in his second letter to Timothy: "And the things you have heard me say in the presence of many witnesses entrust to reliable men who will also be qualified to teach others" (II Timothy 2:2, NIV).

So spiritual multiplication begins, as Paul tells Timothy, by teaching faithful individuals. They in turn will be able to teach others. Here we see four generations of spiritual multiplication: Paul teaching Timothy; Timothy teaching faithful individuals; they in turn teaching others. Through this process, Spirit-filled men and women possess the potential to reach the world with the good news of Jesus Christ in our generation.

A Story of Multiplication

Let me share with you an example of how multiplication has occurred in one church — Fellowship Bible

Church, in Dallas, Texas. When Campus Crusade staff members Norm and Becky Wretland moved there they felt that God had placed them in this church and its neighborhood for a special reason.

"We began to reach out through evangelistic desserts, pool parties and home Bible studies," Norm recalled. "In less than a year, more than 60 of our neighbors have received Christ and our neighborhood is a brand new, exciting place to live."

Dennis Simonetta was one of those who attended one of Norm and Becky's evangelistic desserts. "When I first attended," he admitted, "I wondered what kind of strange party I was going to. Then I saw in these people a quality of life that I hadn't seen before, and they talked about a personal relationship with Jesus Christ. That day I committed my life to Jesus Christ, and I found a new life of love for my family and my neighbors.

"Since then, all of my family have given their hearts to Christ," he said happily. "What a thrill it is to live in a neighborhood full of new Christians and to be a part of helping to share this message right here where we live."

Dennis then began sharing his new life in Christ with a neighbor, Dwight Johnson. "When Dennis first started talking to me about the fact that he had received Christ," said Dwight, "I thought he had flipped his lid. Then I started noticing a change. He didn't come to our drinking parties and nights out with the boys any more. He seemed to love his family more, and I found myself wanting the same thing for my life."

It wasn't long until Dwight received Christ, too — at an evangelistic neighborhood pool party. "Now my wife, son and I have a new life together, full of love for Christ and for each other," Dwight shared. "Now, I, too, have had the privilege of sharing Christ with my neighbors, and it's only a matter of time until our entire neighborhood will be saturated with the claims of Christ."

Dr. Gene Getz, pastor of the growing Fellowship Bible Church in Dallas, was thrilled beyond measure to see Norm and Becky reach out for Christ to those around them and to begin a vital ministry to their neighbors.

"Actually," said Dr. Getz, "about 60 neighbors and children whom they have reached are new members of our church, and we are presently asking God to multiply this strategy throughout all our members. The real key is that Norm and Becky are equipped for the evangelistic and discipleship work of the ministry. This is what we, as pastors, have been commissioned by God to do with all members — equip them for *their* work of ministry."

Beginning with a Vision

The Way of Life Plan, as part of the ongoing strategy of Here's Life, America, is being used to equip many churches to become discipleship training centers to continually train and disciple church members who in turn are involved in reaching the specific neighborhoods, colleges and business areas with the gospel.

As we have explained the Way of Life Plan to pastors around the country, many have begun to catch a vision of the church's fulfilling its purpose of spiritual multiplication through evangelism and discipleship. The success of the Way of Life Plan depends upon the pastor. For, without a vision on his part, the church can never become a discipleship training center. Proverbs 29:18 tells us, "Where there is no vision, the people perish" (KJV).

Many of these pastors have committed themselves to leading the Way of Life Plan in their churches. Because of their personal involvement, the plan has gone beyond being just another program — it has become a movement that is still growing and multiplying.

The key to the plan's longevity lies in building leadership into the movement. Just as Jesus began His earthly ministry by selecting and challenging 12 men while at the same time challenging the multitudes, so have the pastors in the Way of Life Plan begun by selecting and challenging a leadership core of individuals.

These core group members are selected during their Way of Life training. They begin by first attending a three-day introductory seminar. Next, the pastors work with this group for 14 weeks for approximately three and a half hours per week. The pastors continue training their group in discipleship and evangelism, building close personal relationships with these individuals.

They also begin helping them to meet their spiritual needs in a second course which runs eight weeks, one and a half hours, one night per week. Pastors guide them in times of sharing and conversational prayer, Bible study, and review and practice of the skills learned in the first training phase. Following this, the members become trainers or team leaders for new Way of Life groups of two or three persons.

Pastors See Ongoing Impact

A pastor in the South prayerfully searched for a way — a plan — by which to train his people for winning souls to Jesus Christ. Finally, two men from this ministry went to see him and explained Here's Life and the Way of Life Plan. He recalled, "I began to see a concept of multiplication — not just addition to our church, but multiplying in the kingdom of God, beginning small with a leadership core group."

As more of the plan was explained by our two representatives, he began to sense that this was an answer to his prayer. "This is it," he thought. "This is what God wants us to do. God wants us to get into the Here's Life movement."

Another pastor, the Rev. Willie Richardson of the Christian Stronghold Baptist Church in Philadelphia, explained what God has done in his church through Here's Life, America training.

"We began the Way of Life Plan in our church during January 1975 with a leadership core of 10 men whom I began to systematically disciple. We set a goal to share Christ with 1,000 people during 1975. In no other year had we shared the gospel with more than 100. God answered our prayers — we shared the gospel with 1,071 people last year, and of these, 417 prayed and received Christ. Now people in our church are sharing their faith as a way of life. Only five had been doing that at the beginning of the year.

"We added 65 active members to our church last year, and the Sunday morning worship service attendance grew by 25%," Rev. Richardson reported. "Eighty percent of our members regularly attend Sunday school. Members of our original leadership core now lead six discipleship groups in our church."

Here's Life, America and the Way of Life Plan came along just at the right time, according to Wayne Wolchek, pastor of the Westwood Christian Church in Madison, Wisconsin. "When you see an entire congregation suddenly come alive and begin sharing Christ as a way of life after they had taken the training and had had a taste of what it was like to share Christ — this is exciting! Overall it brought the congregation closer together. It has trained them to share Christ and to really enjoy their Christianity and their personal relationship with Christ."

In the Ankeny Baptist Church in Des Moines, Iowa, 85% of its active adult and youth members went through Here's Life, America training, according to the pastor, Bob Tolliver. Most of these individuals went on to participate in the city's "I found it!" campaign. As a result, nearly one out of three people they contacted who had the opportunity to do so prayed and invited Christ into their hearts.

These pastors, like so many others, began to see how the Way of Life Plan provided them with the tools for equipping their people to help carry out the Great Commission. It provided them with a plan in which they could involve their members in a personal ministry of discipleship which not only enabled them to reach others for Christ but also caused them to grow as a strong New Testament church.

Strengthening Churches

The Way of Life Plan is strengthening churches because, as members become involved in sharing their faith, every other facet of their interaction within the church is strengthened as well. Their giving, their prayer life, their Bible study, Sunday school, worship service — everything is strengthened.

The program has brought a surge of joy among people in many churches because for the first time in their lives many of them are beginning to understand what it really and truly means to live a Spirit-filled life by faith and to be a consistent witness for our Lord.

Dr. Charles Stanley, pastor of the First Baptist Church of Atlanta, explained what has happened there since the inception of the program: "Each Thursday evening our people are out sharing their faith, following up those who have made commitments. Sunday after Sunday, we are welcoming into our fellowship people who have made decisions for Christ. We see them being baptized and becoming involved in our discipleship and evangelism classes."

Discipleship Training Centers

Once pastors complete initial training of their leadership cores, the next step is to establish a Discipleship Training Center. These centers give other church members the opportunity to be trained in evangelism and discipleship and to apply their training weekly in a neighborhood outreach team. In a short time exciting transformations begin to take place.

Totally committed pastors begin training and teaching their people, helping the laymen to join them in doing the evangelizing and discipling. This is the way God describes the role of His Church. In His Word, He explains:

"Some of us have been given special ability as apostles; to others He has given the gift of being able to preach well; some have special ability in winning people to Christ, helping them to trust Him as their Savior; still others have a gift for caring for God's people as a shepherd does his sheep, leading and teaching them in the ways of God.

"Why is it that He gives us these special abilities to do certain things best? It is that God's people will be equipped to do better work for Him, building up the church, the body of Christ, to a position of strength and maturity; until finally we all believe alike about our salvation and about our Savior, God's Son, and all become full-grown in the Lord — yes, to the point of being filled full with Christ.

"Then we will no longer be like children, forever changing our minds about what we believe because someone has told us something different, or has cleverly lied to us and made the lie sound like the truth. Instead, we will lovingly follow the truth at all times — speaking truly, dealing truly, living truly — and so become more and more in every way like Christ who is the Head of His body, the church. Under His direction the whole body is fitted together perfectly, and each part in its own special way helps the other parts, so that the whole body is healthy and growing and full of love" (Ephesians 4:11-16).

Dr. Sam Coker recalled what took place at his church: "Before, I wanted to be in charge of or in control of whatever was happening. Now I know that once they're trained, once they learn to walk in the Spirit, God does the controlling. And I just continue to train in this leadership core."

All across America, thousands upon thousands of laymen who have been through the Lay Institute for Evangelism, then in leadership cores in their local churches, are continuing to develop neighborhood groups for Bible study and fellowship. They are witnessing as a way of life — many for the first time are actively going out into the communities to share the gospel, and they are winning others to Christ and introducing them into the fellowship of the church.

Members of the leadership core never "graduate." Instead, the pastor continues to meet with and disciple them through a minimum involvement of a one-hour meeting per week. The cycle of introductory training is repeated with new Way of Life teams being formed. Intermediate and Advanced Discipleship training is offered to Way of Life team members. Leadership core members are committed to meet with and disciple new team leaders so that the leadership multiplication continues to work.

Reaching the World

All across the country I have repeatedly seen small groups of men and women grow spiritually, then begin to multiply into more groups within their church, with each member reaching out into the community with the good news of Jesus Christ.

But the Great Commission is challenging us not to be

content with just reaching our communities, but to go and make disciples of *all nations*. Consequently, the vision of Here's Life, America extends far beyond the community of the local church. It focuses attention on reaching the world.

Each local church, having adopted the Way of Life Plan, becomes a model and center of influence for other churches in reaching communities and entire cities as a part of Here's Life, America.

I am repeatedly told of the excitement of Christians who are involved in this movement — which includes believers from all denominations: Baptists, Presbyterians, Episcopalians, Methodists, Lutherans, Pentecostals and many others — not in a competitive campaign or organization, but in fellowship and in a cause for Christ to claim their cities. As one pastor expressed it, "All of a sudden we found ourselves kind of like the New Testament church — a group of believers claiming a city for God and working in harmony to reach it."

For these Christians and thousands more who have received training through the Here's Life, America movement, sharing the claims of Christ and discipling new believers has become a *way of life*.

Why not share the challenge of the Way of Life concept with your members, if you are a pastor, or, with your pastor, if you are a lay person. Volunteer your availability to help. Make this plan work in your church, and write to me for additional information.

11
Training Disciples

When we began sharing with pastors and laymen the vision God had given us for Here's Life, America, the concept was greeted enthusiastically. But the question was often asked, "How will it be done?"

Though Campus Crusade would not attempt to reach the nation with the gospel by its efforts alone, the task of motivating and training pastors and laymen to help reach America's 215 million people was unprecedented and seemed nearly impossible to some observers.

There had been 200 years of evangelism in this country, and the Great Commission had never been fulfilled. How then was Here's Life any different from other plans or movements?

There has never been a shortage of Christians to communicate God's love to their communities. There has been no problem, either, in supplying them with materials with which to communicate that love. The problem has been how to train enough believers to effectively share their faith so that every American can hear the gospel. How do you train millions of people in personal evangelism?

That ingredient for training — which had been missing for the fulfillment of the Great Commission in this nation in previous generations — is now available. And this training played a major role in the miracle of the Here's Life, America movement.

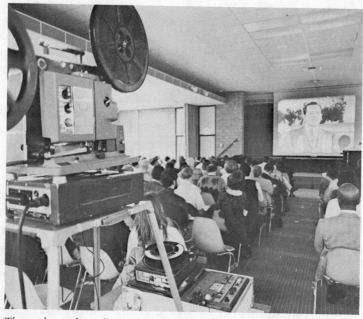

Through mediated training, millions of Christians learned to effectively share the gospel.

At the time God impressed us to pray and believe Him for the fulfillment of the Great Commission in the United States by the end of 1976, we didn't understand how He would do it. We had the capability of training tens of thousands of people through our staff workers, but not the hundreds of thousands who would be needed to saturate this nation with the gospel. Then, in early 1974, in the providence of God, this program, called "mediated training," was a gift of the Lord to us.

Most Significant Breakthrough

What is mediated training? It is the concept of teaching through the use of 16mm film, color slides and cassette tape sound track, together with teacher and student manuals of specific instruction. It is the most significant breakthrough in the history of Campus Crusade for Christ.

The idea of mediated training was first suggested to me and to our staff in 1974 and was later developed by Dr. Norman Bell, a Christian professor of educational psychology at Michigan State University. Dr. Bell and our leaders were eager to see used for the cause of Christ top-flight techniques of mediated instruction that had been developed recently in the secular world.

When I heard the idea while speaking at Michigan State, the Holy Spirit confirmed that this was the answer to our prayer for the salvation of tens of millions in the United States. Such revolutionary concepts as "How to Be Filled with the Spirit" and "How to Witness in the Spirit," plus how-to's of evangelism, could be made available to millions of Christians. We would no longer be limited to our staff as trainers, but laymen and pastors could train others by using the mediated training package.

See, Hear and Practice

Now mediated training is a tried and proven technique for training disciples. The format follows this pattern: the trainee sees a short film vignette which explains the importance of a particular spiritual truth or Christian concept. A film message, designed to explain that truth, follows on such topics as "How to Walk in the Spirit." Immediately after the film, a slide/tape session employs a workbook to review the film content to make certain the trainee retains the key points of the film. He sees a particular concept on a slide and writes the idea in his notebook.

This basic mediated training package takes 14 hours to complete, including a witnessing experience in the local community. This witnessing time immediately implements the spiritual principles learned during the sessions. Those who attend the mediated training study the same basic materials which have proved so revolutionary in changing lives for many years through Campus Crusade's training seminars conducted in churches around the world.

In the formulative days of mediated training, we did not know whether or not such a presentation could really be as effective as a live teacher. But we soon found it to be superior. The tremendous potential of the training became very obvious. Actually, many pastors and lay members tell us they are drawn to the Here's Life movement because of the training in the effective how-to's of communicating the gospel.

"Too many people believe that the gospel should be shared only by the pastor," commented consulting engineer Tom Cady, who participated in the training given in his church. "The training helps lay men and women overcome their inhibitions and shows them how to challenge others to make a commitment to Christ."

Amazing Potential

Larry Marks, a Methodist layman from Athens, Alabama, who recently took the mediated training course, shared: "Personally I was amazed at the amount of information I gained and could recall when I needed it."

He went on to tell how others profited in a remarkable way when the mediated package came to Athens. He particularly delights in telling about a 14-year-old boy who attended the mediated training with him. That weekend the two went witnessing together to apply what they had learned.

"We went into one house," remembers Larry, "and I talked with the wife while this boy talked to the husband. After a while I heard this 14-year-old voice say, 'Lord Jesus, I need You . . .' and this 52-year-old voice follow with, 'Lord Jesus, I need You . . .' Tears came to my eyes as I realized the boy was leading this man to the Lord. It was difficult for me to continue, but I did, and the woman also prayed and received Christ."

Mediated training gave them the ability to remember what to say and do. When they came to a place where they would normally wonder what to say, their training gave them the necessary knowledge to know what to say.

Such memory ability among mediated training "graduates" is not by chance, since the trainee learns through several methods simultaneously. At the same time that he sees a concept on the screen, he hears it on the sound track and fills in blanks or answers questions concerning that concept in his seminar student handbook. For some, self-quizzes — conducted with a latent image developer on specially treated paper — also heightened the learning process.

Based on the findings of Dr. Bell and university surveys, and confirmed by the results of our training programs to date, it is estimated that 80% of the program's students retain 80% of the material. Such a figure stands head and shoulders above results from traditional lectures — where retention averages five percent. It is believed that this mediated training package is the only training of its kind in the Christian world, and we are dedicated to making it available to the churches and other Christian movements.

Training Backbone of Here's Life

Mediated training is the backbone of Here's Life, America. It is the tool used to train pastors and laymen in the Way of Life plan for discipleship. It includes mediated training as its introductory course and follows with two consecutive 13-week study series of intermediate and advanced courses. It has been used to equip telephone and block workers to share the gospel in all of the cities participating in the Here's Life movement. Without this vital gift from God, we could never have adequately trained enough people to effectively saturate the nation with the gospel. To date, nearly 400 sets of mediated equipment have been used to train more than 300,000 people in Here's Life, America.

Phoenix, Arizona, provides a good example of mediated training's indispensable role within Here's Life, America. One staff couple, together with many volunteers, were able to mobilize 105 churches and train 10,000 members for telephone evangelism and home visitation.

Kermit Sutherland, the lay director in Phoenix, gives thanks to the Lord for the marvel of mediated training. "All that's happening in Phoenix wouldn't be happening without it," he told us.

A pastor stated that he believed that mediated training will continue to play a big role in an ongoing program of evangelism and disciple-building in Spokane, Washington. Keel Dressback, pastor of the First Evangelical Free Church, said, "I think that an awful lot of pastors were really surprised at how effective mediated training was in training their people. In a short time, these people were effectively trained, and I think that that's going to have an impact in the days to come as we pursue ongoing discipleship and evangelism."

At the individual level, the local church level and the national level, mediated training displays extraordinary potential as a tool to promote discipleship and evangelism. The mediated training program has already helped train people to visit many of the 70 million families in our nation — both by telephone and door-to-door. Thus, I believe that this method of training Christians will make a significant contribution to taking the gospel to the world as tens of thousands of trained laymen, pastors and students go from the United States to other parts of the world. They will use the mediated training package in other languages, adjusting it to other cultures, as a basis for their work.

Of course, there are large segments of the world that are presently closed to the gospel, but I believe that God has other tools available to us, like mediated training, to allow us to reach them — perhaps the use of satellites or mass distribution of literature.

I believe that, when we obey the impressions of the Holy Spirit and launch out to do what we know is God's will, according to Scripture, He will always give us the means to accomplish what He tells us to do. I believe that by 1980 we will see the Great Commission fulfilled throughout the world. How it will happen I do not know. But our God has been in the miracle-working business through the centuries — parting the Red Sea, causing the walls of many Jerichos to crumble and multiplying the loaves and fishes. Today, as through the centuries, He is looking for men and women who will trust and obey Him.

12
Reaching Out
Through the Media

In November 1976, residents of Seattle, Washington, began noticing billboards popping up around the town with the phrase, "I found it!" on them. In Miami, residents noticed the same phrase plastered on bumper stickers all over town. People in Cleveland saw others wearing "I found it!" lapel pins. TV viewers in Los Angeles switched their TV sets on to see a television special and numerous spot advertisements proclaiming the same slogan. And, in May 1977, New Yorkers saw "I Found It! — New Life in Christ!" flashing out across all of Times Square from a giant advertising screen.

From Alaska to Miami and from Hawaii to New York, and in some 200 cities in between, four-week media campaigns were taking place during 1976 and into 1977. An estimated 179 million people were exposed to the "I found it!" TV commercials and the hour-long TV special. This represents 89% of the people in the United States.

Some 85.6 million, including many of the same people, were also exposed to the "I found it!" slogan through the mass media of radio and newspaper advertising, billboards, bumper stickers and lapel buttons. Feature stories on the "I found it!" campaign appeared in hundreds of major newspapers and national magazines, the total readership amounting to tens of millions of people.

In response to the media campaign, more than two

million incoming calls were received in 217 telephone centers, with more than 800,000 people requesting copies of the "I found it!" booklet. In addition, many millions of phone calls have gone out from the telephone centers, and millions of personal contacts have been made through door-to-door evangelism and in spontaneous personal contacts. There is no human way to document and record what the Holy Spirit has done and is doing through the hundreds of thousands of trained workers. However, it is reasonable to assume that millions of Americans have found new life in Christ as a result of the Here's Life movement.

Communicating Through the Media

A para-professional at an elementary school in Nebraska wore her "I found it!" button in the classroom, whereupon her students asked what she had found. After obtaining clearance from the principal and approval from the children's parents, she devoted time after school hours to sharing the "I found it!" booklet with the inquiring students — several of whom prayed and received Christ.

A young Here's Life, America worker in Madison, Wisconsin, was seen putting an "I found it!" bumper sticker on her car and was asked by a passerby what she had found. The worker shared how she had found a new life in Jesus Christ, then shared the gospel as contained in the Four Spiritual Laws. The inquisitive passerby, upon being exposed to the gospel, prayed and committed her life to Christ. The worker then invited the girl to attend church with her the following Sunday, which she did — accompanied by her husband.

A man in El Paso, Texas, who found a new life in Christ, immediately used the Four Spiritual Laws booklet to share the gospel with 10 other people and prayed with them as they invited Christ into their lives.

After seeing "I found it!" billboards in the states of Iowa and Wisconsin, a traveling salesman finally telephoned an "I found it!" telephone center to satisfy his curiosity. After the telephone worker shared how he had found new life in Christ and presented the gospel through the Four Spiritual Laws, the salesman, standing in a cold,

113

public telephone booth, felt the warm glow of God's love as he prayed and received Christ.

In one large city, a woman television and radio time-buyer for Here's Life, who had been a professing Christian for many years, discovered that through the power of the Holy Spirit within her, God freed her from the bondage of alcoholism. She helped to saturate her area with the "I found it!" campaign.

Bill, an editorial reporter for a large New York news-paper, wrote a feature story on Here's Life, New York. The morning the story ran, Bill called Dick Burr, executive director of Here's Life, New York, whom he had inter-viewed. He apologized that the story was so short (the editors had cut it considerably). Then Bill said, "That little booklet you gave to me — I sat up late last night reading it and looking up the passages in the Bible. I just want you to know that reading that booklet changed my life. I have never felt so good as when I awakened this morning. I've found a new life!"

Miraculous Use

In scores of cities across the nation, people were becoming exposed to the "I found it!" slogan. As an NBC-TV newsman commented to Indianapolis television viewers one night, "By now, everyone in Indianapolis knows that 'I found it' is a personal relationship with Jesus Christ." And so it was in city after city throughout the country. The mass communications media were being used miraculously of God to reach the hearts of millions of people with His love expressed through the person of Jesus Christ.

Regardless of the method of communication — whether by television, by word of mouth, the gospel, when shared faithfully, is always accompanied with power and the Holy Spirit, according to I Thessalonians 1:5 and evi-denced by my personal experience and observations.

Mass Communications in Scripture

The Bible is a veritable treasure house of illustrations of how God has used mass media to communicate His

Through billboards and bumper stickers, as well as lapel pins and newspaper, radio and television advertisements, "I found it" became America's famous phrase.

message to man. When God chose to give His laws to the nation of Israel, He chose a mass communications technique by writing the laws on stone tablets for Moses to show to the people. The prophet Habakkuk, who was given a vision from God, was told, "Write my answer on a billboard, large and clear, so that anyone can read it at a glance and rush to tell the others" (Habakkuk 2:2).

Perhaps the best illustration of God's use of the mass media lies in the Bible itself. The Bible has been published in more translations and in more languages and in greater quantities by far, than any other book in history. God enabled His children to utilize the medium of the printed page to multiply His Word so that hundreds of millions upon millions of people might come to know Him in a personal way through His Son.

But even before the advent of the printing press, the Bible was copied over and over again by hand so that God's Word would be available for more people to read and live by. The apostle Paul and other early leaders in the Church wrote letters to groups of believers in local churches throughout the then known world. Some of those letters are, of course, now contained within the New Testament.

Jesus also used mass communications methods and techniques to convey the truth to the masses. He quoted from the Old Testament, thus multiplying God's original communication. He spoke often in parables, thus dramatizing practical principles to heighten their retention by the listeners. He spoke to large masses of people, many times performing miracles to get their attention — as illustrated by His multiplying of the loaves and fishes.

Certainly the printed Word of God is not an impersonal document. Christians should communicate effectively through the media without resorting to trickery or other means born out of insincerity or ulterior motive.

The Uses of Mass Media

At Campus Crusade, we see mass media tools as having three uses: for evangelism, discipleship-training and motivation. In the Here's Life, America movement, we incorporated all the practical, available communications tools into a total strategy for the saturation of cities with the "I found it!" message. God has given us these communications tools to bring us in contact with the multitudes of people whose hearts He has prepared to hear the gospel.

We use a number of tools for evangelism. In every television special there is more than one opportunity for the viewer to receive Christ. Invitations to receive Christ are given during the half-time program of our televised Athletes in Action basketball games. We have a progressive program for producing evangelistic films, books, cassettes, publications and literature.

Thus far in the Here's Life, America movement, as I have already mentioned, over 322,000 people have been trained for evangelism and discipleship — a task that could not have been humanly possible had God not given us the ability to utilize the modern communication tools of mediated training. Because of these methods and techniques of training, many thousands of men and women are being equipped to live fruitful Christian lives, including sharing their faith in Christ with others.

We also utilize mass communications to motivate Christians to become disciples and to become involved in God's work, to become part of His solution for the world, to live godly lives and to share Christ as a way of life.

The mass media arm of Campus Crusade, under the leadership of Chuck Younkman, is continually evaluating innovations in communications methods and techniques for use by this ministry. Two exciting media of potential usefulness to us are video-discs and communications satellites. Played on equipment that attaches to ordinary TV sets, video-discs offer low cost audio-video program capability for use in the home, at church and school. Communications satellites offer us the technology through which to beam the gospel via radio and TV signals with simultaneous translations throughout the whole world.

Media's Openness

The current public acceptance of Christianity — thanks in no small part to the favorable publicity generated over President and Mrs. Jimmy Carter's faithful witness for the Lord — has had a positive influence on the news media's openness to the message of evangelicals. *Newsweek* in the fall of 1976 published a special issue on "The Evangelicals." *The Saturday Evening Post* devoted its entire April 1977 issue to Christianity. That same month, *Redbook* published the results of its religious survey of 65,-000 women.

Numerous secular magazines began exploring the virtues of Christianity, sometimes by profiling Christian personalities. Sportwriters have been featuring testimonies of one Christian athlete after another in publications ranging from weekly newspapers to national magazines, such as *Sports Illustrated.*

NBC aired in the United States the two-segment, six-hour long, "Jesus of Nazareth" — an $18 million motion picture with an international cast that depicted Jesus Christ as the Savior of the world and the Son of God. This film is being released for viewing in many countries to hundreds of millions of viewers.

The Genesis Project — the most remarkable undertaking in history to film the entire Bible from Genesis to Revelation — is currently being produced at a cost of $280 million. Imagine the impact for God that can be made on a world that is more than 50% illiterate when God's truth is dramatized on film!

The Genesis Project film is historically and theologically accurate. Through it, hundreds of millions of people will hear the Word of God, the gospel of our Lord Jesus Christ, via satellite through simultaneous translations in all the major languages of the world. This is God's doing! To Him be all the glory and praise.

Media Availability: How Long?

But will the media always be so open to communicating positive messages about our Lord and His cause? From all indications, I am sorry to say, probably not. Already, we find that all major networks and many TV and radio stations have policies against selling prime time for Christian programming. Many magazines likewise refuse to sell advertising space for Christian messages.

The pendulum seems to have nearly reached the extent of its swing in favor of Christians utilizing the media, and it could well be swinging back to the side of discrimination against Christian things. Therefore we must take advantage of every opportunity now available to us to reach the masses through the media with the good news of our Lord Jesus Christ.

Two-fold Communications Ministry

Campus Crusade, with a staff of more than 6,000 and many thousands of volunteers, is serving our Lord in 88 countries and 20 protectorates on every continent. We are committed to utilizing the mass communications media for the glory of Jesus Christ and for the training of other Christians in such usage in every country of the world.

We are in urgent need of experienced men and women to fill staff vacancies in all areas of mass communications. We need writers, artists, printers and people skilled in producing programs for television and radio. We offer frequent on-the-job training in mass communications for college students and professors, whether or not they have had previous experience.

Encouraged by the fruitful results of our television and film efforts, we are asking God to provide us with the necessary funds to expand this phase of the ministry to enable us to reach additional millions with evangelistic programming and discipleship training. Ask God to show you how you might have a part in bringing our Christian TV programs to your community and to the world.

Jesus said, "Go into all the world and preach the gospel. . . ." And, now, thanks to Him for the gifts of mass communications media, we have the potential of fulfilling His Great Commission in this generation.

13
Life After Here's Life

Here's Life, America was born as a vision from God when a small group of God's children began to pray and believe God for the fulfillment of the Great Commission, beginning in the United States. It was nurtured by the successes of God-directed campaigns in the pilot cities of Atlanta, Dallas and Nashville. And it has been the catalyst for a national movement among mobilized churches. Now it has developed into a worldwide movement.

The impetus for Here's Life, America has been the "I found it!" media campaigns that saturated the populations of cities with television and radio spots, billboards, bumper stickers, splashy newspaper ads and even lapel buttons.

Now, in more than 200 cities, the "I found it!" campaigns have officially drawn to a close. Yet, in many cities, Christians refuse to let the impact die down. In Columbus, Ohio, for example, new bumper stickers have cropped up on cars and in phone booths: "You can *still* find it!"

Phase Two: The Next Step

In April 1977, Here's Life, America city coordinators, working with local pastors and lay men and women, launched Phase II of Here's Life, America — a continuing strategy of discipleship and evangelism.

Here's Life, America Phase II is designed to help cities reach four critical objectives: (1) to encourage ongoing programs of training in evangelism and discipleship; (2) to encourage continuing city-wide prayer efforts with prayer chains and prayer fellowships; (3) to increase the vision of lay people to reach other cities and countries with the "I found it!" strategy; and (4) to sponsor momentum-building events which would act as evangelistic catalysts.

"We want to give the workers continuing opportunities to share their faith," noted Bob Stark, national Here's Life, America administrator, "and to challenge them and the many new Christians to a deeper level of commitment to Christ.

"Human nature tends to run in cycles," Bob Stark said as he explained how Phase II had developed. "Any time you participate in something like a campaign, you need relaxing time; a time to re-group your thoughts and gain a new perspective on where you're going. We've done this, and now we're ready to continue."

Enthusiastic Response

And the churches were ready, too. Phase II was enthusiastically received when it was introduced in January 1977 at a west coast Here's Life conference at Arrowhead Springs. Two hundred city coordinators, pastors, laymen and their wives attended from 92 cities. Today hundreds of congregations across the country are already participating in Here's Life, America Phase II.

Typical of those who invested their time and talents in the ongoing movement of discipleship and evangelism within their community are John Cook and his wife, Jo, of Decatur, Alabama. They are devoting 30% of their time to Phase II — time away from their successful business. Serving as northern Alabama coordinator, John also is a member of the coordinating committee for the Southeast United States region for Here's Life, America. Jo is enlisting the members of many churches in northern Alabama in the church prayer strategy.

121

Neighborhood Discipleship Strategy

Participating churches are accomplishing their objectives through the Neighborhood Discipleship Strategy for the local church. This strategy contains key ingredients of the "I found it!" campaign — such as telephone evangelism — but without the supporting media advertising.

In addition to making evangelistic contacts encouraged by a new mediated training program in telephone evangelism, laymen are receiving 10 weeks of in-depth training in such areas as follow-up, discipleship and how to conduct neighborhood Bible studies. New believers are being encouraged to become involved in the fellowship of the worker's local church, resulting in church growth.

Christian Leadership Training Center

In Philadelphia, Campus Crusade staff member Carl Combs formulated the idea of the Christian Leadership Training Center while preparing for the Here's Life, Philadelphia media campaign, which took place in May 1976. "When we started working with pastors, I realized that in industry there is continuing education on how to do the job. But there are few places a pastor can go to get continuing practical education. We had a meeting with a group of pastors, and the curriculum for the Christian Leadership Training Center grew out of the needs which they identified."

Ken Stoll, then the new pastor of the Suburban Grace Brethren Church in Philadelphia, was one of the pastors who met with Carl and expressed a desire for establishing a discipleship ministry. "I had to face the fact that I didn't know how to disciple men," he admitted. "I needed to learn."

Pastor Stoll was one of the pastors who participated in Campus Crusade's first Christian Leadership Training Center 30-week course, begun in September 1976. The program is in full operation today, giving continuing assistance to pastors and churches in the area of discipleship and evangelism. The program also calls for each trained worker to reach 60 homes in a neighborhood on a continuous basis with the good news of Jesus Christ.

The Rev. Willie Richardson, pastor of Christian Stronghold Baptist Church in Philadelphia who participated in Here's Life and the Christian Leadership Training Center, reported the effect this has had on his church. He stated that in the past two years — during the "I found it!" campaign and Christian Leadership Training Center — his church has increased in membership from 135 to 260. The budget has quadrupled. The Way of Life evangelism and discipleship ministry in his church has prepared 15 people who are now in full-time Christian service. They have seven evangelistic teams led by seven men who never before were in leadership positions. And, at each mid-week prayer meeting, attendance is over 100 people.

The Rev. Rick Clark, of the Oreland Baptist Church in Philadelphia, reported, "As a direct result of my training at the Christian Leadership Training Center, our church has grown 130% in only six months."

The Rev. Nathaniel Winslow of the New Testament Church of Christ shared that his church has tripled in size within one year.

The goal of the Christian Leadership Training Center in Philadelphia is to mobilize 300 churches by 1980 to saturate their city with the gospel. This will result in the training of 20,000 workers who will share the gospel with every home in Philadelphia at least once a year.

The city of Philadelphia was chosen as a pilot city for the Christian Leadership Training Center to assist pastors in planning a program of discipleship and evangelism in their churches. Soon this basic training will be available to all interested pastors in every city and community in America.

Worldwide Impact

We anticipate that the ongoing Here's Life movement in Philadelphia and many more cities will grow to have a worldwide impact. We are encouraged that this will become a reality because, among other things, of the strategy's "Adopted City" program. Ron Blue, Here's Life,

America Phase II executive coordinator, explained it at the recent Arrowhead Springs conference: "There are only 89 cities — mostly smaller ones — which haven't had Here's Life, America campaigns, and we've encouraged the present Here's Life city coordinators to 'adopt' all of these unreached cities."

More and more city coordinators are responding to this challenge. And, as commitments of this type are made, we are seeing that laymen are eager to pray for their adopted city, willing to help recruit pastors and church workers and locate financial support.

Moreover, I believe that many city coordinators will be impressed by God to "adopt" other *countries* through making commitments calling for prayer and financial support. I am persuaded that the reason God has so blessed our great nation is that we, as His servants, might use our God-given resources and abilities to communicate the gospel to the entire world.

So, as the unofficial bumper stickers remind us, "You Can *Still* Find It!" And we are praying and believing God that by faith millions more will find an abundant new life in Christ through the ongoing ministry of thousands of local churches as they continue their participation in Here's Life, America Phase II.

I anticipate in all confidence in God's faithfulness that the unprecedented spiritual awakening we have already seen through Here's Life, America and many other individuals and movements will be surpassed by far in future weeks and months and years as more and more Christians are trained to share their faith in Christ and commit themselves to discipling new believers as a way of life.

14
An Unprecedented Spiritual Awakening

For the past 25 years I have been actively involved in national and worldwide evangelism — on planning and executive committees or responsible organizationally for great evangelistic thrusts. Working with thousands of local churches and many Christian organizations, our staff of more than 6,000 in 88 countries and 20 protectorates have seen God touch the lives of millions of people on every continent. But what God is doing today through His Church and His individual servants and organizations is 100 times — yes, 1,000 times — greater than anything I have ever seen or read about in the almost 2,000-year history of the Church. I do not refer to the Here's Life movement only but to hundreds of other expressions of God's love to man.

Increasingly in the past few years, God has raised up many servants and movements to present the good news to the entire world in an unprecedented way. For example, Billy Graham has been used of God for more than 30 years to influence millions for Christ. Now God has raised up many others.

Ben Armstrong of National Religious Broadcasters reports that 125 million Americans listen to Christian radio and television programs each week. Robert Schuller, W.A. Criswell, Oral Roberts, Jerry Falwell, Rex Humbard, Richard De Haan, Leighton Ford, Pat Robertson, Theodore Epp, Oswald Hoffman and many others preach the gospel of Jesus Christ each week to tens of millions. The seed which they and thousands of other godly pastors have been sowing so faithfully for years has taken root and is now ready for the harvest. Here's Life, America is one of the vehicles which God is using for the most phenomenal spiritual harvest in the history of the church.

Results Beyond Measure

The question is frequently asked, "What were the results?" First of all, Here's Life, America provided only the impetus for a movement which has not ended — and by God's grace its influence will not end until Jesus Christ returns! And He is delaying His return in order that more people will have a chance to receive Him (II Peter 3:9).

The harvest before us is even greater than what we are now experiencing. Our reports from the field are estimated to represent from 40% to 60% of actual results in the *first* level of discipleship alone. Once the four-week, official "I found it!" media campaign has ended, reports of continuing evangelism and discipleship are no longer made. It is reasonable to believe that many of the people who participated in the Here's Life mediated training program are continuing to win others to Christ and disciple them.

In order to evaluate and refine the Here's Life strategy, representative samplings of the movement's results have been and will continue to be made both by our staff and by outside research teams which will evaluate the effectiveness of Here's Life on a continuing basis. The findings, though preliminary as of this writing, are quite revealing. For example, we have learned that increase in church membership (among mainline, evangelical denominations) in affected areas is not a valid indicator of the movement's effectiveness.

It appears that as many as half the people who made decisions for Christ were already members of churches, thus their conversions do not show up in membership increases at their churches. We have learned, too, that not all unchurched new believers are joining local churches right away.

Strengthening the Local Church

One of the major objectives of Here's Life is to encourage church growth and spiritual vitality and maturity. We seek to do this by helping to strengthen the local church through a continuing movement of discipleship and evangelism. In the process, we have discovered that new converts do not always flock into the church immediately after receiving Christ. No doubt the real lasting results of Here's Life in terms of church membership will not be accurately measured for several years.

For example, a few days ago a brilliant young man, who had a Ph.D. in business management, shared with me how some years ago he had received Christ through an emphasis similar to Here's Life. He witnessed to the fact that he had received assurance of his salvation at that time and his life was changed. However, he did not really become active in a local church and begin a faithful, fruitful witness for Christ until five years later.

According to many involved in local and mass evangelism, this may be the rule rather than the exception. For example, Dr. Billy Graham often states that the real success of his city-wide crusades cannot be adequately determined for at least five years.

I was personally influenced and discipled for Christ through a local church. Thus, from the beginning of the Campus Crusade ministry, we have strongly emphasized the need to encourage new, as well as old, believers to become actively involved in a local church, to be baptized and to participate regularly in the fellowship and leadership.

But we can only encourage new Christians to become active in a local church. We recognize that many who have found Christ through Here's Life are for the present being fed in home Bible studies. Others are receiving spiritual nourishment through sermons and Christian programs on TV and radio. Many of these are already witnessing for Christ and are introducing others to Him. However, they have not yet understood the importance of joining a local church.

127

The Church on TV

We live today in a television culture. As you well know, there are several excellent Christian sermons and church programs on radio and TV each Sunday morning and in some areas throughout the week. Some of these have such a strong appeal that millions of Americans worship God in the privacy of their homes. My mother and father — now approaching 90 years of age and no longer able to attend their local church — can hardly wait for the spiritual feast which they receive each Sunday morning. They regularly listen to from three to six of their favorite television preachers.

We must recognize that the only way we can woo people away from the attractive series of inspiring Sunday morning TV worship services is to give them something much better in the local church. Not to do so will result in a growing indifference to the importance of the local church.

Though I am grateful to God for the many excellent Christian radio and TV programs, and my comments should not be interpreted as criticism, I feel that we can be more effective in discipling Christians through the fellowship of a local church, provided it is truly equipped to do so. That is why Phase II of Here's Life is so very important.

We are finding, too, that those new believers who do join local churches after receiving Christ oftentimes — for a variety of reasons — join weeks, months or even years later.

Then there are new believers who previously belonged to churches where Christ was not the center of their worship. As a result, they became disenchanted with churches in general, thinking them all alike. Yet, many of these people are often very zealous for our Lord. We would be in great error to assume that their conversion is not valid just because they do not attend one of the churches of our choice.

A survey of many churches following the media campaign has confirmed the obvious. Those churches with an active, warm, friendly, outgoing, Christ-centered fellowship where the Word of God is faithfully preached in the power of the Holy Spirit are experiencing immediate and sometimes phenomenal results.

However, those churches which expected the new converts to come crowding in without any special effort on the churches' part are predictably disappointed with the "results" of Here's Life. But Here's Life, America also affected those who already were church members. The North Long Beach Brethren Church reported, ". . . Many of our adults who have been stagnant for years came alive and have been continuing to share their faith."

Reaching Out

It is quite likely that millions of men and women have made commitments of various kinds and degrees to the Lord Jesus Christ as a result of the Here's Life, America campaign, but only the Lord will ever know who they are or what those decisions have been. However, we are already hearing all kinds of reports of how people have made decisions and later those decisions have surfaced and individuals are beginning to come into the fellowship of the church after having made commitments months before. For example, Buma Sorrell of the Bellevue Baptist Church, Memphis, Tennessee, made this report:

"Six months after being involved in the 'I found it!' campaign in Memphis, I had an exciting experience. I was a part of our church's soul-winning group, God's Invasion Army. We went out to make a call and knocked on a door, expecting to see a young woman who had visited our church. We found only her husband at home and, knowing absolutely nothing about his spiritual condition, we proceeded to share with him the Four Spiritual Laws. He was very warm and open. There was no indication of his position until we came to the two circles and I asked him which one represented his life. He immediately smiled and said, 'The one on the right. I am a new Christian. Jesus Christ has come into my life.' I said, "That's great. Can you tell us about it?'

"He began to share with us about his life before Jesus. Before Jesus, he was a struggling, country western singer and had been the full route — even had been an alcoholic.

129

somehow he had not been able to get it all together and he could not deal with the sin in his life.

"One evening he turned on his television set and saw a special program, sponsored by Here's Life, America, with Dean Jones, Carol Lawrence, Chuck Colson, Bill Bright and others. He was very touched by the testimonies, and when they explained how he could receive Christ as personal Savior, he asked Jesus to come into his life and Jesus did just that. 'It was wonderful,' he said. He was able to conquer drinking immediately and he had such peace and joy. However, since he did not call the number flashed on the television screen, no follow-up material or visit resulted to encourage him in his growth. Now, we knew why God had led us to him and we praised God for His goodness.

"We had the privilege of sharing with him a need for a public profession of faith, baptism and church membership. The next Sunday, we met him and his wife for services at our church. His wife made her decision a few weeks after he made his as a result of his changed life and a message she had heard by our pastor on television. During the invitation, they both responded to Dr. Adrian Rogers' call to make public profession of their faith in Jesus as Savior and Lord. A week later they were baptized and are now experiencing growth through our church."

This is an example of what is happening and will continue to be duplicated in tens and hundreds of thousands of cases in the months and years to come, as a result of the Here's Life, America "I found it!" campaign.

Correcting Anti-church Attitudes

One very important fact is becoming increasingly clear: We who love the church and are committed to its growth and greater influence in society must recognize and take immediate steps to correct the long standing anti-church attitudes which are still prevalent and strong. Multitudes are being drawn to Jesus Christ but for various reasons are still not convinced of the relevance of the church. Churches which are experiencing little or no growth must be willing to learn from churches which are church. Churches which are experiencing little or no growth must be willing to learn from churches which are experiencing rapid and solid growth.

The statistics which we have received are, for the most part, from surveys taken immediately after the "I found it!" media campaigns and therefore do not reflect the subsequent results of the ongoing outreach. But based on these surveys we are able to report what probably represents only the "tip of the iceberg" of what God has really done and is doing.

Media Response: An estimated 179 million people will have been exposed to the "I found it!" television commercials and two one-hour TV specials. This represents 89% of the people in the United States. In addition, 85,639,-000 people were exposed to the intensive four-week, "I found it!" media campaign which utilized, along with TV and radio, newspaper ads, billboards, bumper stickers, lapel buttons, posters and other means of communication.

Of those exposed to the "I found it!" media campaign, 68,460,000 were made aware that this slogan refers to finding a personal relationship with Jesus Christ, and they were offered an opportunity to receive a free booklet telling them how they could find it, too.

More than 2 million phone calls were received in 217 telephone centers, and more than 800,000 people requested copies of booklets.

Neighborhood Campaigns: Reports from more than 251,000 campaign volunteers showed the following results: 6.5 million personal contacts, more than a half million people expressed a desire to receive the Lord Jesus Christ as their Savior and more than 66,500 people enrolled in Bible studies in local churches.

Unrecorded Results: There were three areas which represent occasions when individuals made commitments for Christ, but because of the unique circumstances, no record was available. While it is impossible to determine the quantity of responses from these areas, the total could well be in the millions.

The two television specials presented God's love and forgiveness in Jesus Christ to the viewing audience, and opportunities were provided to receive Christ. Most who made decisions did not indicate them.

Furthermore, many churches indicated that, as preparation for their participation in the Here's Life, America campaign, the Four Spiritual Laws were shared with entire Sunday school classes and in some cases with entire congregations. Based upon our experience in training hundreds of thousands in many churches, we estimate that 10 to 50% of those who heard the gospel presented through the Four Laws to their various church groups made decisions for Christ. Such figures were not reported to Campus Crusade for Christ.

Finally, no records are kept of the more than 300,000 Christians who were trained to share their faith in Christ spontaneously as a way of life. Hundreds of churches have already used the Here's Life, America campaign to begin ongoing evangelism and discipleship programs as they continue to share God's love as a way of life.

Though the actual recorded decisions immediately following the media campaign were 543,000, it is reasonable to assume, on the basis of the immediate recorded results of the media campaign and the personal follow-up, that literally millions of people have responded positively to the "most joyful news ever announced."

A Look Ahead

The first phase of Here's Life, America placed a strong emphasis on evangelism, resulting in an unprecedented response. Phase II, which was launched in April 1977, places a strong emphasis on discipleship and follow-up of both new and older Christians in all churches which desire to participate, as well as a continued emphasis on evangelism. Phase III, for 1978 and thereafter, calls for an expanding emphasis on discipleship and evangelism through the local church, including the use of the mass media.

Yet, our Lord commanded His children to "go into *all* the world, make disciples of *all* nations and preach the gospel to *all* men." In obedience to His command, we launched Here's Life, World in early 1977.

15
Worldwide Hunger for God

I am often asked, "Why are so many people receiving Christ as their Savior and Lord through the Here's Life, America movement?" To me the answer is obvious: There is an incredible hunger for God. Basically, everyone, whether or not he acknowledges it, is hungry for God. We were created that way.

As St. Augustine wrote centuries ago, "Thou hast made us for Thyself, O God, and our hearts are restless until we find our rest in Thee."

Jesus said: "No man can come unto Me, except the Father who sent Me draws him" (John 6:44, KJV), and God, through His Holy Spirit, is drawing multitudes to our Savior. Though a person may turn from God and, in his ignorance, may seek fulfillment and a meaningful life through personal achievement in business or a profession or through attainment of worldly goals — making money, using drugs or alcohol, involvement in immoral sex, whatever — there is still a universal hunger for God, and it is no accident. It is a condition that God, out of His perfect love, has given to every person.

How Can They Hear?

It is God's will that "anyone who calls upon the name of the Lord will be saved" (Romans 10:13). However, the apparent dilemma remains: "But how shall they ask

Him to save them unless they believe in Him? And how can they believe in Him if they have never heard about Him? And how can they hear about Him unless someone tells them? And how will anyone go and tell them unless someone sends him?" (Romans 10:14,15).

The answers are obvious. Jesus Christ has given the command to all Christians to "go and make disciples in all the nations" and share the good news with all men (Matthew 28:19,20).

From the inception of Campus Crusade, our staff have been committed to helping fulfill the Great Commission of our Lord in this generation. Here's Life, America and Here's Life, World are strategies to help reach this goal which have evolved through God's guidance in the more than a quarter of a century since the inception of this ministry.

Prepared Hearts

I am constantly encouraged, as I travel this nation and the world, to see and hear how the Holy Spirit is working in the hearts of multitudes in such unprecedented and revolutionary ways — so much so that one can truly say that there is a worldwide hunger for God.

Numerous surveys taken in countries where the gospel can be freely proclaimed lead me to believe that one can reasonably conclude that at least one out of two persons would receive Christ this very moment if they could hear a simple, clear-cut presentation of the gospel given by a properly trained, Spirit-filled person.

This would not hold true in the hard-core Muslim world, nor in Israel at present, nor in certain parts of Europe and the United States. But the fact that in some countries 80 to 90% of those confronted with the invitation of our Lord respond positively to the gospel would lead us to conclude that an overall one out of two persons is a reasonable estimate.

God, in His love and mercy and through the power of His Holy Spirit, has prepared multitudes to hear the truth of the gospel and to receive Jesus Christ — even the hearts of those who might disclaim any hunger for God. This is

People everywhere are hungry to know God.

because hearing the gospel can ignite a spiritual flame in even the coldest of hearts.

For more than 30 years I have assumed that most people who are not Christians would like to be if given an opportunity to receive Christ. This is a principle I have seen work in miraculous ways time and time again — and especially during the Here's Life, America campaigns in cities around the country.

For example, I was told about a nurse in a Palm Beach, Florida, hospital who bent over a sleeping 85-year-old woman patient to adjust her oxygen supply. The nurse accidently pricked herself with her "I found it!" lapel pin, awakening the elderly woman with an "Ouch!"

"What did you find?" the awakened patient asked as she saw the "I found it!" pin.

Then the nurse shared the good news of Jesus Christ with her. In a few minutes the woman prayed with the nurse and received Christ. Then, almost immediately, the elderly woman's eyes closed and she went to be with the Lord.

In another city, a young telephone worker named Patsy dialed a "wrong" number. Undaunted, she began sharing Christ with the man who answered, only to discover that he was at that very moment on the verge of murdering his wife, then committing suicide. After three meetings with a trained counselor, the man prayed and received Jesus Christ as Savior and Lord.

Producing Fruit

This same hunger for God was present in the first century. The apostle Paul wrote, "The same Good News that came to you is going out all over the world and changing lives everywhere, just as it changed yours that very first day you heard it and understood about God's great kindness to sinners" (Colossians 1:6). Yet, we realize that while we have the privilege to be bearers of the good news of Jesus Christ, it is the Holy Spirit who changes lives.

Paul elsewhere explained, "For when we brought you the Good News, it was not just meaningless chatter to you; no, you listened with great interest. What we told you pro-

136

duced a powerful effect upon you, for the Holy Spirit gave you great and full assurance that what we said was true" (I Thessalonians 1:5).

In both cases the Colossians and the Thessalonians received Christ the first time they heard the gospel. Likewise, Paul wrote to the church in Rome: "Dear Friends in Rome: This letter is from Paul, Jesus Christ's slave, chosen to be a missionary, and sent out to preach God's Good News. This Good News was promised long ago by God's prophets in the Old Testament. It is the Good News about His Son, Jesus Christ our Lord, who came as a human baby, born into King David's royal family line; and by being raised from the dead He was proved to be the mighty Son of God, with the holy nature of God Himself.

"And now, through Christ, all the kindness of God has been poured out upon us undeserving sinners; and now He is sending us out around the world to tell all people everywhere the great things God has done for them, so that they, too, will believe and obey Him" (Romans 1:1-5).

God has created us with the same kind of attraction on the part of our spirit to the wooing of God as is the attraction of iron to a magnet.

Yes, across the entire world there is a hunger for God that only God can satisfy. The psalmist wrote, "For He satisfies the thirsty soul and fills the hungry soul with good" (Psalms 107:9).

Abundant Life

I can say categorically, on the basis of interviewing literally thousands of people over a period of 30 years, that no nonbeliever I have ever met has experienced the kind of life that God has ordained for His children to live. Those who walk in faith and obedience are promised and enabled to live a full and abundant life by Jesus: "I am come that they might have life, and that they might have it more abundantly" (John 10:10, KJV).

The great cry of the centuries and the cry of multitudes from over the earth today is, "How can I experience this full and abundant life? How can I know God in a vital, personal way?"

We are told that there are 85 million people who attend church across America every Sunday, and yet our surveys indicate that over one half of them are not sure of their salvation — not certain that they will go to heaven when they die. We often find that from 10 to 70% of the membership of a local church have such doubts. On the basis of previous training experiences, it is reasonable to believe that as many as 20% of the more than 300,000 people who were trained during the time of the Here's Life, America campaigns received assurance of salvation during their training!

One pastor of a church of 1,500 members was skeptical of these figures. He volunteered to survey his own congregation and found to his surprise that 70% of his people were not sure of their salvation. Two Sundays later, the ushers distributed the Four Spiritual Laws booklets to each member of the congregation. That morning the pastor read the contents of the booklet as his sermon. He asked those who wished to receive Jesus Christ as their Savior and Lord to read the prayer aloud with him as he prayed. He reported that most of them prayed!

"This is the greatest day of my ministry and in the history of this church!" he exclaimed.

Many other pastors have followed the practice of reading the Four Spiritual Laws and the companion booklet, "Have You Made the Wonderful Discovery of the Spirit-filled Life?" to their people as their sermons for a worship service as the members read along with them from their own booklets. The results have been phenomenal.

Importance of Faith

After some years of counseling with many people, I became aware in a dramatic way of the importance of faith in the assurance of salvation. As the Scriptures remind us, "For by grace are ye saved through faith; and that not of yourselves; it is the gift of God; not of works, lest any man should boast" (Ephesians 2:8,9, KJV).

This discovery was brought home to me when a man

studying for his doctoral degree at the University of California, Los Angeles, received Christ. Shortly afterwards, he wrote to his parents in Zurich, Switzerland, to tell them that he had become a Christian. He mentioned my name in the letter as the one who had helped him, which prompted his parents to respond by writing to say that they, too, wanted to become Christians and asked for an appointment to talk with me personally.

They flew nearly 8,000 miles — all the way from Switzerland — for the appointment! And as they sat in my office, they asked how they could receive Christ, too. I explained the gospel to them, including why Christ died on the cross for our sins and the power of the resurrection. I read John 1:12, which states: "To all who received Him, He gave the right to become children of God." Then I shared Revelation 3:20 in which Jesus promises, "Look! I have been standing at the door and I am constantly knocking. If anyone hears Me calling him and opens the door, I will come in and fellowship with him and he with Me."

"If you want to become Christians," I said to the young man's parents, "You must ask Jesus to come into your heart, forgive your sins and change your life."

"We ask Jesus into our lives everyday, sometimes many times a day," the father replied. "But we are still not sure that He has heard us. How can we know for sure that He is with us?"

Saved Through Faith

Suddenly, I had nothing to say, because they were already doing what I was recommending and still they were not sure of their salvation. Silently I prayed, "Lord, please help me; I don't know what to do or what to say."

Immediately the Lord impressed upon me that I should share Ephesians 2:8,9 with them. Though I had used this passage on many occasions, I suddenly saw the real truth of it for the first time in my life! "For by grace are ye saved through *faith* . . . !" It was not enough to receive Jesus, not enough to ask Him to come into one's life; one had to *believe* through faith that Jesus would do what He promised. Through faith, one can say, I believe that if I open the door of my life to Jesus He will come in. Through faith, when I receive Christ, I know according to the promises of God that I will become His child.

As I explained this truth to the parents of my student friend, they responded immediately. The light went on. They had assurance of their salvation!

Through the years following this experience, I have discovered that thousands of people with whom I have counseled had the same problem. As I have shared with them the simple biblical truth concerning the importance of faith, the Holy Spirit has given them complete assurance of their salvation.

EXPLO '74

One of the most dramatic confirmations of this truth was illustrated when I was speaking on Ephesians 2:8,9 at EXPLO '74 — a special week of training in discipleship and evangelism sponsored by Campus Crusade for Christ and held in Seoul, Korea. Delegates were there from every community of South Korea and from 78 other countries.

I had discovered through personal experience and counseling with Korean pastors and missionaries on several previous trips that there were many Koreans who lacked assurance of their salvation.

I shall never forget the phenomenal impact of that experience. Imagine speaking to crowds night after night that ranged in number from an estimated 750,000 to 1.5 million, according to official Korean estimates. It was an overwhelming experience to share the most joyful news ever announced with the largest crowds in history.

In one of my messages, I explained to the Koreans how they could be sure of their salvation, how they could be sure they would go to heaven when they died. I read to them the promises of God, recorded in John 1:12, Ephesians 2:8,9 and Revelation 3:20. I told them that if they had prayed to God and had asked Jesus Christ into their lives over and over again, but were still not sure of their salvation, that they could, in faith, be sure before they left the meeting that night. At the end of my message — which was translated by one of God's choicest anointed servants, Dr.

C.C. Park, the gracious pastor of the famous Young Nak Presbyterian Church in Seoul with 18,000 members — I asked those who were not sure of their salvation and eternal destiny to bow and pray silently after me, phrase-by-phrase.

"Lord Jesus," I began, "I need You. I open the door of my life and receive You as my Savior and Lord. Thank You for forgiving my sins. Take control of my life. Make me the kind of person You want me to be."

After praying with that vast multitude I explained to them that, if they had prayed that prayer with me in faith and meant it, they would never need to pray it again. According to Ephesians 2:8,9, they had been saved by faith. By faith, they could say, "I believe that Jesus will do what He promised. I can know that He has come into my heart because He said He would. I know that I have become a child of God and that my sins are forgiven because the Word of God promises that. I know that I will go to heaven when I die because the Word of God promises eternal life to all who receive Christ."

"Right now," I told them, "you can thank the Lord Jesus that He is in your life and that He will never leave you, as He promised (Hebrews 13:5).

"Tonight," I said, "if for the first time in your life you are sure that when you die you will go to heaven, if this is the first time that you can confidently say, 'I know for sure that I'm a child of God, that my sins are forgiven, I'm on my way to heaven,' will you stand, right now, as an expression of your faith?"

I challenged them in this way because God is pleased by such an expression of our faith. The Bible says, "Without faith it is impossible to please God" (Hebrews 11:6, NIV). Within moments it seemed as if everybody were standing! As far as the eye could see they were standing — and the crowd extended for approximately a mile.

Later, about midnight, Dr. Joon Gon Kim, director of Campus Crusade in South Korea and EXPLO '74, phoned to tell me that, according to their estimates, at least 90% of the people had responded to the invitation. He reported that apparently more than a million people indicated that

An estimated 1.5 million people attended one rally at EXPLO '74 in Korea — a spiritual reawakening that is now spreading around the globe.

they had received Christ!

Though my heart was filled with praise to God over the phenomenal response, I was nevertheless skeptical: Did all the people who responded really understand what I had said? Were they simply standing because others around them had stood? Were they responding to the emotions of the moment?

My skepticism was greatly relieved when later during the week of EXPLO '74, Dr. Kim surveyed 10,000 of the more than 300,000 Korean delegates who participated in the week-long training conference. More than 84% indicated that they had received assurance of their salvation during the week of training. Now, I was assured that more than one million people had indeed responded with understanding and assurance to my invitation to receive Christ.

For years I have prayed that I would have a part in introducing hundreds of millions to my wonderful Lord. As I saw that vast throng respond to the gospel and heard Dr. Kim say, "More than a million responded when you gave the invitation to receive Christ tonight," God seemed to say to me, "You have been praying for hundreds of millions to receive Christ; now, tonight, you have seen how quickly a million could be reached. Your prayers for hundreds of millions will be answered."

Obviously, I do not expect hundreds of millions to receive Christ through the ministry of Campus Crusade for Christ alone, but through many individuals and movements and churches uniting in a great concerted effort such as Here's Life, America and Here's Life, World. God will do it!

The EXPLO '74 trainees went out the following Saturday afternoon for a two-hour sharing session that covered almost every block in the city of Seoul. Nearly two-thirds of them had reported back by evening, indicating that they had talked with 440,000 people and that 274,000 of them had prayed and received Christ! Our hearts still overflow with gratitude to God for the privilege of seeing so many hungry souls for the Lord brought into the kingdom that day.

How to Know You Are a Christian

Perhaps you, like many of these wonderful Korean people, ask Jesus into your life again and again in times of emotional crises or in response to a moving presentation of the gospel. Yet nothing seems to happen in your life. There are two possible reasons:

First, some ask Jesus into their lives without realizing that He is not just a mere man, a historical figure, Jesus of Nazareth, but He is the God-man — both God and man, the Savior, and promised Messiah, who died for our sins and was buried and on the third day was raised from the dead. He is the living Lord of life and history and has the power to change the life of any and all who receive Him. When one "receives" Him superficially just because others are receiving Him, without understanding who He is, nothing is likely to happen.

Second, some people do not ask the Lord Jesus to come into their lives as an expression of faith. They insult Him by asking Him in again and again. Ask Him to be your Savior once and thereafter thank Him daily as an expression of faith that He is in your life, for He has promised never to leave nor forsake you.

To be sure that you are a Christian you must be aware, intellectually, of certain basic truths:

First, God loves you and has a wonderful plan for your life.

Second, man is sinful and separated from God; thus he cannot know and experience God's love and plan.

Third, Jesus Christ is God's only provision for man's sin. Through Him you can know and experience God's love and plan.

And, fourth, we must individually receive Jesus Christ as Savior and Lord; then we can know and experience God's love and plan.

But it is not enough to merely ask the Lord Jesus Christ into your life. You must have *faith*. You must believe that He will enter according to His promise. Again, I quote from God's Word, "For by grace you have been saved through *faith*, and that not of yourselves, it is the gift of

God; not as a result of works, that no one should boast" (Ephesians 2:8,9, KJV).

Jesus said, "Behold, I stand at the door, and knock; if anyone hears My voice and opens the door, I will come in to him, and will sup with him, and he with Me" (Revelation 3:20, KJV).

In John's Gospel, we are told, "But as many as received Him, to them He gave the right to become children of God, even to those who believe in His name" (John 1:12, KJV).

Does all that I have shared with you make sense? Have you ever personally received the Lord Jesus Christ as your Savior? If you have received Him, do you have the assurance of your salvation? Are you sure that if you died right now, you would spend eternity with God in heaven?

If you cannot answer "yes" to these questions, may I suggest that you bow right where you are and receive the Lord Jesus as your Savior.

If you have never received Christ by a definite, deliberate act of your will, you can do so now, in prayer. And if you are not sure you are a Christian, you can make sure now. In either case, I suggest that you pray this or a similar prayer of faith, making it your very own:

"Lord Jesus, I need You. I thank You for dying for my sins. I open the door of my life and receive You as my Savior; I want to serve You as my Lord. Thank You for forgiving my sins and for giving me eternal life. Take control of the throne of my life. Make me the kind of person You want me to be. Amen."

Did you just now ask Christ into your heart? Then where is He right now in relation to you? You can be sure, if you prayed that prayer sincerely, that the living Christ now dwells in you and that you have eternal life. That is His promise, and He will not deceive you.

"And what is it that God has said? That He has given us eternal life, and that this life is in His Son. So whoever has God's Son has life; whoever does not have His Son, does not have life. I have written this to you who believe in the Son of God so that you may know you have eternal life" (I John 5:11,12).

The decision to receive Jesus Christ as your Lord and Savior is absolutely the most important one you will ever make in your life. Now that you are sure you are a Christian, share your faith and assurance with others as a way of life!

Write to me and tell me of your decision. I will mail special literature to you that will help you begin your new life in Christ. You will find a handy reply card in the back of this book. Fill it out and mail it to me today.

16
Here's Life, World

America, unlike any other nation in history, began its Christian heritage at the very founding of the Republic. The Declaration of Independence and the Constitution of the United States affirm that this nation was raised up by God to fill a unique role in His great plan for man. Most of our first 100 colleges and universities, including Harvard, Princeton, Yale, Dartmouth, Columbia and many others, were established as Christian institutions. In fact, according to the Thomas Jefferson Research Institute, 90% of the curriculum of our schools in the year 1776 was based on the moral and spiritual teachings of the Word of God.

There has never been another nation, apart from Israel, so spiritually blessed of God as has been the United States. Neither has there been one so materially blessed. With only 6% of the world's population, we possess 54% of all the world's wealth. It has been estimated that America owns more than 80% of the Christian wealth and has 75% of the world's trained Christian workers.

Why has God given such spiritual and material abundance to Americans? I believe that it is because many of our founding leaders were godly people who dedicated this nation to Jesus Christ. But what would be the consequences to us if we should misuse these blessings of God?

Warning from Prophecy

Some people see an ominous warning voiced in the prophecy of Revelation, chapter 17, concerning the people of the end-time society called Mystery Babylon. Instead of using the wealth and resources given to them by God for His service in ministering to other nations, they began using their material blessings to satisfy their shameful materialistic appetites. Eventually, Mystery Babylon, according to the prophecy, will turn its back on God completely and follow Satan's antichrist. Just as ancient Rome fell through moral and spiritual decadence, so will end-time Babylon — and so will any other nation that follows this same path of self-gratification which leads to inevitable destruction and judgment.

Unless we recognize that God has blessed us as individuals and as a nation in order that we might share His love and forgiveness in Christ with the rest of the world, we must incur God's chastisement upon us, as did ancient Israel.

We should take to heart the admonition of the prophet Ezekiel as he spoke to his generation which had already sinned beyond the point of no return. This, in my opinion, is not yet — nor does it need to be — true of the United States and Canada. "Throw away your money! Toss it out like worthless rubbish, for it will have no value in that day of wrath. It will neither satisfy nor feed you, for your love of money is the reason for your sin. I gave you gold to use in decorating the Temple, and you used it instead to make idols! Therefore, I will take it all away from you. I will give it to foreigners and to wicked men as booty. They shall defile My Temple. I will not look when they defile it, nor will I stop them. Like robbers, they will loot the treasures and leave the Temple in ruins" (Ezekiel 7:19-22). Many believe that if we continue to sin against God as did ancient Israel, God will use an atheistic nation to destroy us, as in Ezekiel's warning to Israel.

We, in America, should take such prophetic warnings seriously. We need a change in our priorities. Instead of using our God-given wealth for our own pleasure we need to invest it — along with our time and talent — in helping to reach the world for Christ in obedience to our Lord's command. For God will not continue to pour out His great blessings upon this nation if we consume them for ourselves in order to indulge in lives of ease and luxury or to build large estates for our heirs and tax-free foundations. All that we have is a gift from God and should be used for His glory.

Jesus warns, "Don't store up treasures here on earth where they can erode away or may be stolen. Store them in heaven where they will never lose their value . . ." (Matthew 6:19).

Let me hasten to say, however, that many Christians are diligently seeking God's will for their lives and for our nation. They have learned to trust God for the principle given in the Gospel of Luke: "Much is required from those to whom much is given, for their responsibility is greater" (Luke 12:48). Thank God for individuals whom He has gifted with the ability to make money and who are using it for His glory while they are still alive to see that it is well invested for His purposes — the winning and discipling of men and women for Christ.

Every investment for our Lord should be more carefully weighed than a business investment. A wise investor places his money where it will earn the greatest possible return on his investment. Money invested for our Lord and His kingdom should be invested where it will accomplish the most for His glory in terms of the number of disciples built and the number of people introduced to Christ.

The Greatest Challenge

When our Lord Jesus Christ gave the greatest challenge ever given to man in the form of the Great Commission, He gave it to you and to me and to all Christians. But not only did He give us the Great Commission; He also has given us, especially in the United States and Canada, the money, the manpower and the technology to take the gospel to the entire world by the end of 1980, if only we are willing to pay the price.

Around the world I ask the question of Christians: "What is the greatest thing that has ever happened in your life?" To which, without exception, the answer is: "To know Jesus Christ as my Savior and Lord." Then the second question logically follows: "If knowing Christ is the greatest thing that has ever happened to you, what is the greatest thing that you can do for other people?" And the answer is always the same: "To help them to know Christ."

Thus, God has given us in North America the unique and unprecedented ability to share Christ with the world. We must not abandon the spiritual victories and territories we have gained. We must continue to build disciples — spiritual multipliers — and through them saturate our nation and the world with the gospel. Every year our country needs to be saturated with the good news of Jesus Christ and every generation must continue what has been begun.

The task is not completed. There are tens of millions of people who have not yet received Jesus Christ as their Savior and Lord. There are tens of millions more who are still baby Christians — some of whom have been Christians for 25 or 50 years or more, but are still spiritual babies. The fulfillment of the Great Commission is a continuing process. We must continue to do what we are now doing and ask God to enable us to do much more.

Reaching the World for Christ

We must motivate and encourage one another to help reach the rest of the world for Christ in obedience to His command. Ninety-three percent of the world's population lives outside the United States and Canada. Our Lord has commanded us to go to them with the good news of His love and forgiveness. We have the most advanced technology in history. We have at least 75% of the trained Christian workers in the world. And, we have at least 80% of the Christian wealth of the world. So, if the rest of the world is to be reached, the Christians of America and Canada must assume a major role in helping to reach it. But the Great Commission was given not only to the church in America — it was given to the universal church, whose members on earth reside in virtually every nation in the world.

This brings us to this ministry's vision to see the

world's more than four billion people reached with the gospel by the end of the year 1980. How will it happen? Humanly speaking, it is an impossible goal. Yet, our Lord commanded that we be obedient and faithful in going to the entire world to share with others "the most joyful news ever announced." He promised that He would be faithful in supplying us with all the ability and all the resources to accomplish the task. Therefore we can expect the fulfillment of His promise: "And the Good News about the Kingdom will be preached throughout the whole world, so that all nations will hear it, and then, finally, the end will come" (Matthew 24:14).

How, then, can we possibly expect God to reach the great country of China with its 800 million-plus population? And the Soviet Union with its 260 million? And all of Eastern Europe with its 126 million? And the entire Muslim world of the Middle East with its 125 million? These are absolutely impossible barriers to overcome, humanly speaking.

Expecting Miracles

There is only one way the church will accomplish the goal of fulfilling the Great Commission by the end of 1980, and that is through dramatic, supernatural intervention by God. I expect that many miracles will demonstrate God's love and power in response to the faithfulness of His children who believe. I expect dramatic changes, even in China and Russia, which will enable the gospel to have free course in those countries. Again, from a human perspective, this is not possible — but neither was the parting of the Red Sea nor the feeding of the 5,000 with a few loaves and fishes.

You see, God is sovereign and all-powerful. He truly does rule in the affairs of men and of nations, and His Word reminds us that a nation is just a drop in the bucket to Him! He truly does love all men and is not willing that any should perish, but that all should come to Christ. For these and many more reasons we should expect Him to honor and bless every effort to obey His command, provided our motives are pure and our objective is to bring greater honor, glory and praise to our Lord.

According to this ministry's plans, the years 1977-1978 are the years in which the Here's Life movement will be launched in at least 100 new countries, on every continent.

Finland was chosen after much prayer to become a pilot nation for Europe. Next would come the city of Berlin, West Germany. Lahore and Karachi, Pakistan, have been selected as pilot cities in the Middle East.

Here's Life, Benoni will be the launching point for the movement on the African continent. Tijuana, Mexico, will be the pilot campaign from which the movement will spread throughout the Central and South American countries. Here's Life has already been launched in several locations in Asia, including India, the Philippines, Taiwan, Hong Kong, Malaysia and Singapore.

The challenge is extremely great in communicating the gospel in so many different cultures and languages. Mass communications technologies and methods vary greatly from one country to another. While TV was a viable vehicle to carry the good news of Jesus Christ to Americans, the medium is nearly non-existent in many developing countries of the world. Thus, other means must be found for communicating to the masses and following up inquiries with personal contact. The message itself must be written and rewritten in many languages, with the many cultural differences taken into consideration. With God's help, the work is being done.

Here's Life, Asia

At the invitation of our Asian director, Bailey Marks, and our national directors in several countries, I took a 13-day trip to five countries in Asia in the spring of 1976. I visited the Philippines, Malaysia, Hong Kong, Singapore and Taiwan — where we launched the Here's Life movement. The enthusiasm for the movement in those countries was even greater than in the United States, if that were possible.

The Lord impressed upon me, through this remarkable response of Asian leaders, that He wanted us as a ministry to be the catalyst for launching Here's Life in

153

most of the free countries of the world before the end of 1978. I saw how easily it can happen — if only we obey and trust God. I spoke to approximately 8,000 people, mostly Chinese. Many of them are praying that one day, soon, they will be able to return to mainland China to share the good news of our Savior and Lord with their fellow Chinese.

Miracles in Kerala

The first Here's Life campaign to be launched outside the North American continent was our Asian pilot effort in the state of Kerala, India. During the year of 1976, God's message of love and forgiveness blanketed Kerala, and the India Campus Crusade for Christ staff are jubilant! The spiritual harvest far exceeded anyone's expectations. Preliminary figures (which could prove to be but a small percentage of the actual numbers) indicate that more than 1.85 million of Kerala's 22 million people made decisions for Christ during the Here's Life campaign!

From the busiest streets of large cities in this southernmost Indian state to the most remote mountainous tea plantations, 43,309 committed and trained Christians walked from house to house bearing the good news of Jesus Christ.

"It began as an impossible dream in 1969," recalls Thomas Abraham, national director of India Campus Crusade for Christ. "But by the grace of God, on December 31, 1976, almost every home (99%) had been contacted."

The results of door-to-door evangelism: 7.7 million opportunities to share the gospel person-to-person, out of which 1.85 million decisions for Christ were made!

In addition, large evening meetings were conducted around the state in order to reach those who were working or attending school during the day. More than two million people attended these meetings, with 380,000 of them indicating they made decisions for Christ!

Training Christians in the basic how-to's of personal evangelism and follow-up, and encouraging them to become involved on a person-to-person basis, was the key to blanketing Kerala, India, with the claims of Jesus Christ.

We rejoice with our India Campus Crusade for Christ staff and jubilant co-laborers over what God has done in Kerala and join with them in praying that Here's Life will now spread to become a movement throughout all of India and across the vastness of Asia with its hundreds of millions of people.

Growing Global Movement

Now, because of what God is so dramatically doing in Asia, as well as the United States and Canada, other countries in Africa, South America, Europe and the Middle East are responding with the same enthusiasm for Here's Life to come to their countries. Sensing that the Holy Spirit is preparing the hearts of millions of Christians the world over for mass evangelism and discipling, I believe that we are on the threshold of a global Here's Life movement that will help to see the Great Commission fulfilled in this generation.

As obedient Christians — whether we live in America or any other country — we need to recognize that our first concern is to make a total commitment of our lives to the living Christ. The apostle Paul explained what we must do: "Give your bodies to God. Let them be a living sacrifice, holy — the kind He can accept. When you think of what He has done for you, is this too much to ask? Don't copy the behavior and customs of this world, but be a new and different person with a fresh newness in all you do and think. Then you will learn from your own experience how His ways will really satisfy you" (Romans 12:1,2).

We are to be mindful that we have but one life and that it will soon pass; none of us is going to live more than another one hundred years, but all believers are going to spend eternity with our Lord. Remember, we can eat only one meal at a time and wear only one suit of clothes at a time.

We can take nothing with us when we die. We can spend our lives just making money and living for personal and selfish pleasures, or we can do what our Lord has commanded us to do: seek first the kingdom of God, set our affections on things above, lay up our treasures in heaven, follow Him, and He will make us fishers of men.

Jesus says, "You prove that you follow Me when you bear much fruit" (John 15:8, NIV). In this way you bring great glory to God.

So I would recommend that every Christian, whatever his country, begin to think strategically about financial investments. Should we invest our money for the cause of Christ while we are still alive, or should we build estates which we will leave to loved ones or foundations? Obviously, the biblical way — God's way — is to invest that which He has given to us while we are still alive in order to accomplish the most in winning and discipling others for Christ.

A Matter of Time and Talents

Recently, Hank Jones, a staff member of several years who has had a remarkable ministry with Christian leaders in Asia, shared with me a passage found in the thirteenth chapter of Acts. There, he pointed out, the church sent the cream of their crop, so to speak, to be missionaries. They sent Paul and Barnabas, their leaders, to start new churches in other cities. We are more prone to send young seminary graduates to the mission fields rather than our most effective and fruitful pastors and mature laymen.

So, we have been impressed to lay before many of the leading pastors and lay people of America a challenge to take a leave of absence from their pulpits and businesses for a month or six months or a year or more, and go to a foreign city to encourage participation in the Here's Life movement. I would suggest that a pastor take with him some of his leading people. Returning from these discipling missions overseas, these pastors will be able to encourage their congregations to continue to pray for the beachheads which they have helped to establish and to provide funds and materials to help saturate their adopted cities with the gospel.

This, I believe, is a concept that merits the involvement of thousands of leading pastors of the world, especially those in the United States and Canada.

This is one of many ways committed Christians can

participate in Here's Life, World. If God is speaking to your heart about doing something to help fulfill the Great Commission throughout the world in this generation, I wish you would write to me and let me know what God is telling you to do.

Let us pray that Christian America will recognize that the spiritual and material blessings that God has showered upon us are not to be misused for our own personal self-gratification, but for doing His work in this country and in all nations of the world.

The Night Cometh

The tides of atheism continue to move rapidly throughout the world. We do not know how much more time we have in which to proclaim the gospel, for already the lamp of freedom has gone out in many countries. We must work now, for "the night cometh when no man can work" (John 9:4, KJV). If we deny this fact, we risk the possibility of losing not only our fortunes, but also our freedom and lives because of our disobedience to Christ.

But if we give ourselves diligently, prayerfully, with total commitment of all we are and have to the glory of God, *now*, He will be pleased; the conditions of II Chronicles 7:14 will be met; and even those countries which now are closed to the gospel will, in my opinion, be opened. Then we, in this generation — yes, by the grace of God, even before the end of 1980 — will see the entire world saturated with the gospel and the Great Commission thus fulfilled.

17
A Personal Challenge

During the six years between 1970, when according to a Gallup poll, only 17% of Americans believed that faith in God was very important, and 1976, when another poll indicated that 56% believed that faith in God was very important, a great spiritual awakening began to spread across our nation.

As previously stated, God has used many people, organizations and movements as participants in this great spiritual awakening. Here's Life, America was one of the ways God chose to speak to approximately 179 million people concerning their need of our Savior. To Him alone be worship, glory, honor and praise! What we have seen and are now seeing is so obviously His doing and, in my opinion, in direct and specific answer to prayer, that no individual or group of people would dare accept the credit.

As we have already stated, when God impressed upon some of His servants in 1968 to pray and work for total saturation of the nation with the gospel by the end of 1976 and the world by the end of 1980, there was no human reason to believe that it could be done. However, in eight short years this miracle of God did take place and a great change in our nation can already be observed. Yet, the best is still before us — the tide of the Spirit of God is once again moving powerfully across America and throughout the world.

Social Changes

Significant social reforms, however, normally follow five to ten years — or even 25 years — after a great awakening. I anticipate that out of the present great spiritual awakening will come major reforms that will affect the lives of everyone in America and much of the world.

For example, I am confident that there will be a considerable decrease in the divorce rate, a lessening of dependency on drugs and alcohol and that the crime rate will be reduced in city after city. I am assured that racial inequities and conflicts will be dealt with and solved in a more equitable, Christian way. The influence of secular humanism in the classrooms of America will be recognized for its contribution to the disintegration of the moral and spiritual fiber of our society and proper corrective measures will be taken. I believe that there will be a greater emphasis on our basic Judeo-Christian heritage. I am looking forward to a dramatic change for the better in upgrading the quality of TV fare and all entertainment.

In the past, the trend in this country has been gradually away from the things of God, and I am confident that there will be a turning back to the things of God as changed people inspired by the love of God will be doing that which pleases Him. We should not expect a sudden confrontation and dramatic transformation, but these changes will come because tens of millions of people at the grass roots level are turning back to God, and their lives are being changed for the better in the process. Changed individuals in sufficient numbers equal changed communities, changed countries and a changed world.

The individual will be the key to social reform. Consequently, Here's Life, America, as a part of this spiritual awakening, can best be appraised in terms of the changed lives of individuals in its long term contributions to a changed world.

"To me," commented Bill Fagan, city coordinator in New Orleans, "Here's Life, America is the suspicious, hostile gang leader now sharing in love his new life in

Jesus Christ. . . . It is the radiant face of a young girl who for the first time experienced the joy of leading another to the Savior. It is the aged, terminally ill woman church leader who came to clearly understand and gain assurance of her salvation through the grace of God. It is my own life and that of my dear family transformed by witnessing an experience of the love and power of the Holy Spirit of God.

"Here's Life, New Orleans has only begun as a movement of evangelism and discipleship, and we're trusting God to make our city a testimony to the glory of Jesus Christ," Bill concluded.

Pressing on Toward the Goal

I rejoice in the many millions of people who have been and will be introduced to our Lord. It is out of a deep sense of love, gratitude and obedience to our Lord and our love for others that we press on toward the goal of helping to reach America and the world for Jesus Christ. The Great Commission reminds us that the greatest thing that ever happened to us is knowing Christ, and the greatest thing we can do to help others is to introduce them to Christ.

Those of us who live in the United States and Canada where the gospel has been freely proclaimed and the masses are already aware of Christ dare not continue to concentrate exclusively on oversaturating our own countries when most of the world has not yet heard the gospel once.

Dr. Oswald J. Smith, famous Christian statesman and missionary, who formerly pastored Toronto, Canada's People's Church, has said that no one has the right to hear the gospel twice until everyone has had the opportunity to hear it at least once. So, those of us who have heard the wonderful story of Jesus and His love over and over again are obligated and privileged to help share it in other lands.

Coupled with this privilege is the availability of a technology that has not existed for any other generation of Christians. Missionaries of 50 years ago often spent their lifetime serving the Lord, only to see a handful of people come to know Christ. Now, because of modern technology, we are able to proclaim the gospel to a third of the world's population at one time via communications satellite. Pope Paul, for example, is reported to have spoken to over 1.3 billion people during the 1976 Christmas holidays.

We dare not miss this incredible, unique, unprecedented opportunity in communications technology for telling the story of Jesus Christ to the world.

Reaching All Nations

God's Word is a command to each and every generation to fulfill the Great Commission. We must bear in mind that a servant does not question the instructions of his master. We in this movement are endeavoring to do, through the enabling of the Holy Spirit, what God has instructed us to do. We are committed to helping tell the world about His love and forgiveness through Jesus Christ. The very fact that we pray and work toward that definite goal of 1980 assures us that there will be hundreds of millions of people who will hear the gospel and many millions will be added to the kingdom of our Lord because of the dedicated servants who have been faithful to obey our Savior and His command.

If, however, we do not attempt to reach these goals, we will be disobedient to our Lord and an unprecedented opportunity for spiritual harvest will be lost. But we are encouraged by Jesus' own teaching that the "Good News about the kingdom will be preached throughout the whole world, so that all nations will hear it, and then, finally, the end will come" (Matthew 24:14). We know that the task of fulfilling the Great Commission will be realized in some generation by Christians committed to this, the most worthy of all objectives. We pray that we might be that generation.

Unfortunately, some Christians have turned their minds from obeying Christ's Great Commission, only to withdraw and wait, unproductively, for Christ's return and the rapture of the Church. Such behavior is unscriptural, as we learn from Christ's own inference when He told his servants to work "for the night cometh when no man can work" (John 9:4, KJV).

161

I believe our attitude should be like that of Martin Luther: "If Christ comes tomorrow, I will plant a tree today." In his statement, we see a responsibility for keeping as our goal the saturation of the world with the gospel — a goal that we are to be praying and working toward as a way of life.

Meeting the Crisis

The wind of heaven is plainly blowing. Carnal, lethargic, fruitless Christians are beginning to awaken from their indifference, and none too soon, for the tide of atheism is running against us. Our precious freedom is in serious jeopardy, and our very lives are at stake. Yet with the various crises there is a growing hunger for God worldwide. However, nothing short of a great spiritual awakening is adequate for the crises that face us.

"Do you think the work of harvesting will not begin until the summer ends four months from now?" asked our Lord. "Look around you! Vast fields of human souls are ripening all around us, and are ready now for reaping" (John 4:35). If that were true when the Lord spoke it, surely it is infinitely more true today. Hundreds of millions of men and women throughout the world, I am persuaded, are waiting to hear the gospel, ready to receive Christ.

God's Word reminds us, as recorded in Romans 10:13-15a, "Whoever will call upon the name of the Lord will be saved. How then shall they call upon Him in whom they have not believed? And how shall they believe in Him whom they have not heard? And how shall they hear without a preacher? And how shall they preach unless they are sent?"

A Personal Challenge

Is God speaking to your heart through the reading of this book which is filled with reports of God's miraculous love and power in the lives of many? If so, I earnestly appeal to you, as pastor or lay person, to dedicate your life, from this moment forward, to the urgent task of praying and working for spiritual awakening in your church, community, nation and the world. Your total commitment to

162

our risen Savior and to the fulfillment of the Great Commission which He has given to all believers can be multiplied through Here's Life, America Phase II and Here's Life, World.

During the Bicentennial, I visited Independence Hall in Philadelphia. There, I saw a copy of the Declaration of Independence. Again I was reminded that the men who signed that document did so at the risk of their lives, their fortunes and their sacred honor. For they knew that in the eyes of the King of England and the authorities they were traitors and would be hanged as such should the colonial cause fail.

In like manner, I appeal to you urgently and earnestly to pledge your life, fortune and sacred honor for the cause of Christ and His Church, for the triumph of freedom and the fulfillment of our Lord's command to make disciples of all nations and preach the gospel to all men.

I encourage you to become or to continue to be involved in the Here's Life, America movement through your local church. Ask your pastor how you can assist him in serving Christ in your church and community as a part of Here's Life, America Phase II.

By the grace of God and the enabling of the Holy Spirit, as millions of Christians of all denominations throughout the world meet the conditions of II Chronicles 7:14, our nations will be turned back to God, and we shall see the Great Commission continue to be fulfilled in the United States and throughout the world in our generation — yes, by the end of 1980.

Conclusion

Two of the most effective tools which God has given to the Campus Crusade ministry and to the Here's Life movement are the booklets, "Have You Heard of the Four Spiritual Laws?" and "Have You Made the Wonderful Discovery of the Spirit-filled Life?"

An estimated 250 million copies of the Four Spiritual Laws and at least 50 million copies of the booklet which explains how to be controlled and empowered by the Holy Spirit have been printed in every major language of the world. It is reasonable to assume that many millions of lives have been changed forever as a result of reading the two booklets. The contents of these helpful booklets are reproduced on the following pages. May I encourage you to read them prayerfully and share them with others.

Have You Heard of the Four Spiritual Laws?

Just as there are physical laws that govern the physical universe, so are there spiritual laws which govern your relationship with God.

LAW ONE

GOD **LOVES** YOU, AND OFFERS A WONDERFUL **PLAN** FOR YOUR LIFE.

(References should be read in context from the Bible wherever possible.)

God's Love

"For God so loved the world, that He gave His only begotten Son, that whoever believes in Him should not perish, but have eternal life" (John 3:16).

God's Plan

(Christ speaking) "I came that they might have life, and might have it abundantly" (that it might be full and meaningful) (John 10:10).

Why is it that most people are not experiencing the abundant life?

Because . . .

LAW TWO

MAN IS **SINFUL** and **SEPARATED** FROM GOD. THEREFORE, HE CANNOT KNOW AND EXPERIENCE GOD'S LOVE AND PLAN FOR HIS LIFE.

Man Is Sinful

"For all have sinned and fall short of the glory of God" (Romans 3:23).

Man was created to have fellowship with God; but, because of his stubborn self-will, he chose to go his own independent way and fellowship with God was broken. This self-will, characterized by an attitude of active rebellion or passive indifference, is evidence of what the Bible calls sin.

165

Man Is Separated

"For the wages of sin is death" (spiritual separation from God) (Romans 6:23).

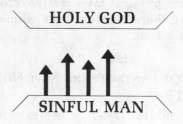

This diagram illustrates that God is holy and man is sinful. A great gulf separates the two. The arrows illustrate that man is continually trying to reach God and the abundant life through his own efforts, such as a good life, philosophy or religion.

The third law explains the only way to bridge this gulf . . .

LAW THREE

JESUS CHRIST IS GOD'S **ONLY** PROVISION FOR MAN'S SIN. THROUGH HIM YOU CAN KNOW AND EXPERIENCE GOD'S LOVE AND PLAN FOR YOUR LIFE.

He Died in Our Place

"But God demonstrates His own love toward us, in that while we were yet sinners, Christ died for us" (Romans 5:8).

He Rose from the Dead

"Christ died for our sins . . . He was buried . . . He was raised on the third day, according to the Scriptures . . . He appeared to Peter, then to the twelve. After that He appeared to more than five hundred . . ." (I Corinthians 15:3-6).

He Is the Only Way to God

"Jesus said to him, 'I am the way, and the truth, and the life; no one comes to the Father, but through Me' " (John 14:6).

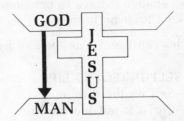

This diagram illustrates that God has bridged the gulf which separates us from God by sending His Son, Jesus Christ, to die on the cross in our place to pay the penalty for our sins.

It is not enough just to know these three laws . . .

LAW FOUR

WE MUST INDIVIDUALLY **RECEIVE** JESUS CHRIST AS SAVIOR AND LORD; THEN WE CAN KNOW AND EXPERIENCE GOD'S LOVE AND PLAN FOR OUR LIVES.

We Must Receive Christ

"But as many as received Him, to them He gave the right to become children of God, even to those who believe in His name" (John 1:12).

We Receive Christ through Faith

"For by grace you have been saved through faith; and that not of yourselves, it is the gift of God; not as a result of works, that no one should boast" (Ephesians 2:8,9).

When We Receive Christ, We Experience a New Birth
(Read John 3:1-8).

We Receive Christ by Personal Invitation

(Christ is speaking) "Behold, I stand at the door and knock; if any one hears My voice and opens the door, I will come in to him" (Revelation 3:20).

Receiving Christ involves turning from self to God (repentance) and trusting Christ to come into our lives to forgive our sins and to make us the kind of person He wants us to be. Just to agree intellectually that Jesus Christ is the Son of God and that He died on the cross for our sins is not

167

enough. Nor is it enough to have an emotional experience. We receive Jesus Christ by faith, as an act of the will.

These two circles represent two kinds of lives:

SELF-DIRECTED LIFE
S—Self on the throne
†—Christ is outside the life
•—Interests are directed by self, often resulting in discord and frustration

CHRIST-DIRECTED LIFE
†—Christ is in the life
S—Self is yielding to Christ
•—Interests are directed by Christ, resulting in harmony with God's plan

Which circle best represents your life?

Which circle would you like to have represent your life?

The following explains how you can receive Christ:

YOU CAN RECEIVE CHRIST RIGHT NOW BY FAITH THROUGH PRAYER

(Prayer is talking with God)

God knows your heart and is not so concerned with your words as He is with the attitude of your heart. The following is a suggested prayer:

"Lord Jesus, I need You. Thank You for dying on the cross for my sins. I open the door of my life and receive You as my Savior and Lord. Thank You for forgiving my sins and giving me eternal life. Make me the kind of person You want me to be."

Does this prayer express the desire of your heart?

If it does, pray this prayer right now, and Christ will come into your life, as He promised.

Have You Made
the Wonderful Discovery
of the Spirit-filled Life?

EVERY DAY CAN BE AN EXCITING ADVENTURE FOR THE CHRISTIAN who knows the reality of being filled with the Holy Spirit and who lives constantly, moment by moment, under His gracious direction.

The Bible tells us that there are three kinds of people:

1. NATURAL MAN
(One who has not received Christ)

"But a natural man does not accept the things of the Spirit of God; for they are foolishness to him, and he cannot understand them, because they are spiritually appraised" (I Corinthians 2:14).

SELF-DIRECTED LIFE
S—Ego or finite self is on the throne
†—Christ is outside the life
•—Interests are directed by self, often resulting in discord and frustration

2. SPIRITUAL MAN
(One who is directed and empowered by the Holy Spirit)

"But he who is spiritual appraises all things . . ." (I Corinthians 2:15).

CHRIST-DIRECTED LIFE
†—Christ is in the life and on the throne
S—Self is yielding to Christ
•—Interests are directed by Christ, resulting in harmony with God's plan

169

3. CARNAL MAN

(One who has received Christ, but who lives in defeat because he trusts in his own efforts to live the Christian life)

"And I, brethren, could not speak to you as to spiritual men, but as to carnal men, as to babes in Christ. I gave you milk to drink, not solid food; for you were not yet able to receive it. Indeed, even now you are not yet able, for you are still carnal. For since there is jealousy and strife among you, are you not fleshly, and are you not walking like mere men?" (I Corinthians 3:1-3).

SELF-DIRECTED LIFE

S—Self is on the throne

†—Christ dethroned and not allowed to direct the life

•—Interests are directed by self, often resulting in discord and frustration

1. GOD HAS PROVIDED FOR US AN ABUNDANT AND FRUITFUL CHRISTIAN LIFE.

Jesus said, "I came that they might have life, and might have it abundantly" (John 10:10).

"I am the vine, you are the branches; he who abides in Me, and I in him, he bears much fruit; for apart from Me you can do nothing" (John 15:5).

"But the fruit of the Spirit is love, joy, peace, patience, kindness, goodness, faithfulness, gentleness, self-control; against such things there is no law" (Galatians 5:22,23).

"But you shall receive power when the Holy Spirit has come upon you; and you shall be My witnesses both in Jerusalem, and in all Judea and Samaria, and even to the remotest part of the earth" (Acts 1:8).

170

THE SPIRITUAL MAN — Some personal traits which result from trusting God:

Christ-centered
Empowered by the Holy Spirit
Introduces others to Christ
Effective prayer life
Understands God's Word
Trusts God
Obeys God
Love
Joy
Peace
Patience
Kindness
Faithfulness
Goodness

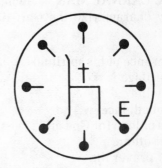

The degree to which these traits are manifested in the life depends upon the extent to which the Christian trusts the Lord with every detail of his life, and upon his maturity in Christ. One who is only beginning to understand the ministry of the Holy Spirit should not be discouraged if he is not as fruitful as more mature Christians who have known and experienced this truth for a longer period.

Why is it that most Christians are not experiencing the abundant life?

2. CARNAL CHRISTIANS CANNOT EXPERIENCE THE ABUNDANT AND FRUITFUL CHRISTIAN LIFE.

The carnal man trusts in his own efforts to live the Christian life:

A. He is either uninformed about, or has forgotten, God's love, forgiveness, and power (Romans 5:8-10; Hebrews 10:1-25; I John 1; 2:1-3; II Peter 1:9; Acts 1:8).

B. He has an up-and-down spiritual experience.

C. He cannot understand himself — he wants to do what is right, but cannot.

D. He fails to draw upon the power of the Holy Spirit to live the Christian life.

(I Corinthians 3:1-3; Romans 7:15-24; 8:7; Galatians 5:16-18)

THE CARNAL MAN — Some or all of the following traits may characterize the Christian who does not fully trust God:

Ignorance of his spiritual
  heritage
Unbelief
Disobedience
Loss of love for God and
  for others
Poor prayer life
No desire for Bible study
Legalistic attitude
Impure thoughts
Jealousy
Guilt
Worry
Discouragement
Critical spirit
Frustration
Aimlessness

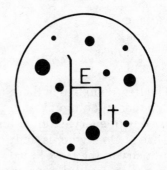

(The individual who professes to be a Christian but who continues to practice sin should realize that he may not be a Christian at all, according to I John 2:3, 3:6, 9; Ephesians 5:5.)

*The third truth gives us the only solution
to this problem . . .*

3. JESUS PROMISED THE ABUNDANT AND FRUITFUL LIFE AS THE RESULT OF BEING FILLED (DIRECTED AND EMPOWERED) BY THE HOLY SPIRIT.

The Spirit-filled life is the Christ-directed life by which Christ lives His life in and through us in the power of the Holy Spirit (John 15).

A. One becomes a Christian through the ministry of the Holy Spirit, according to John 3:1-8. From the moment of spiritual birth, the Christian is indwelt by the Holy Spirit at all times (John 1:12; Colossians 2:9,10; John 14:16,17). **Though all Christians are indwelt by the Holy Spirit, not all Christians are filled (directed and empowered) by the Holy Spirit.**

B. The Holy Spirit is the source of the overflowing life (John 7:37-39).

C. The Holy Spirit came to glorify Christ (John 16:1-15). When one is filled with the Holy Spirit, he is a true disciple of Christ.

D. In His last command before His ascension, Christ promised the power of the Holy Spirit to enable us to be witnesses for Him (Acts 1:1-9).

How, then, can one be filled with the Holy Spirit?

4. WE ARE FILLED (DIRECTED AND EMPOWERED) BY THE HOLY SPIRIT BY FAITH; THEN WE CAN EXPERIENCE THE ABUNDANT AND FRUITFUL LIFE WHICH CHRIST PROMISED TO EACH CHRISTIAN.

You can appropriate the filling of the Holy Spirit **right now** if you:

A. Sincerely desire to be directed and empowered by the Holy Spirit (Matthew 5:6; John 7:37-39).

B. Confess your sins.

By **faith** thank God that He **has** forgiven all of your sins — past, present, and future — because Christ died for you (Colossians 2:13-15; I John 1; 2:1-3; Hebrews 10:1-17).

C. Present every area of your life to God (Romans 12:1, 2).

D. By **faith** claim the fullness of the Holy Spirit, according to:

1. HIS COMMAND — Be filled with the Spirit.
   "And do not get drunk with wine, for that is dissipation, but be filled with the Spirit" (Ephesians 5:18).

2. HIS PROMISE — He will always answer when we pray according to His will. "And this is the confidence which we have before Him, that, if we ask anything according to His will, He hears us. And if we know that He hears us in whatever we ask, we know that we have the requests which we have asked from Him" (I John 5:14,15).

Faith can be expressed through prayer . . .

HOW TO PRAY IN FAITH TO BE FILLED WITH THE HOLY SPIRIT

We are filled with the Holy Spirit by **faith** alone. However, true prayer is one way of expressing your faith. The following is a suggested prayer:

"Dear Father, I need You. I acknowledge that I have been directing my own life and that, as a result, I have sinned against You. I thank You that You have forgiven my sins through Christ's death on the cross for me. I now invite Christ to again take His place on the throne of my life. Fill me with the Holy Spirit as You **commanded** me to be filled, and as You **promised** in Your Word that You would do if I asked in faith. I pray this in the name of Jesus. As an expression of my faith, I now thank You for directing my life and for filling me with the Holy Spirit."

Does this prayer express the desire of your heart? If so, bow in prayer and trust God to fill you with the Holy Spirit **right now.**

HOW TO KNOW THAT YOU ARE FILLED (DIRECTED AND EMPOWERED) BY THE HOLY SPIRIT

Did you ask God to fill you with the Holy Spirit? Do you know that you are now filled with the Holy Spirit? On what authority? (On the trustworthiness of God Himself and His Word: Hebrews 11:6; Romans 14:22,23.)

Do not depend upon feelings. The promise of God's Word, not our feelings, is our authority. The Christian lives by faith (trust) in the trustworthiness of God Himself and His Word. This train diagram illustrates the relationship between **fact** (God and His Word), **faith** (our trust in God and His Word), and **feeling** (the result of our faith and obedience) (John 14:21).

The train will run with or without the caboose. However, it would be futile to attempt to pull the train by the caboose. In the same way, we, as Christians, do not depend upon feelings or emotions, but we place our faith (trust) in the trustworthiness of God and the promises of His Word.

HOW TO WALK IN THE SPIRIT

Faith (trust in God and in His promises) is the only means by which a Christian can live the Spirit-directed life. As you continue to trust Christ moment by moment:

A. Your life will demonstrate more and more of the fruit of the Spirit (Galatians 5:22,23) and will be more and more conformed to the image of Christ (Romans 12:2; II Corinthians 3:18).

B. Your prayer life and study of God's Word will become more meaningful.

C. You will experience His power in witnessing (Acts 1:8).

D. You will be prepared for spiritual conflict against the world (I John 2:15-17); against the flesh (Galatians 5:16,17); and against Satan (I Peter 5:7-9; Ephesians 6:10-13).

E. You will experience His power to resist temptation and sin (I Corinthians 10:13; Philippians 4:13; Ephesians 1:19-23; 6:10; II Timothy 1:7; Romans 6:1-16).

SPIRITUAL BREATHING

By faith you can continue to experience God's love and forgiveness.

If you become aware of an area of your life (an attitude or an action) that is displeasing to the Lord, even though you are walking with Him and sincerely desiring to serve Him, simply thank God that He has forgiven your sins — past, present and future — on the basis of Christ's death on the cross. Claim His love and forgiveness by faith and continue to have fellowship with Him.

If you retake the throne of your life through sin — a definite act of disobedience — breathe spiritually.

Spiritual breathing (exhaling the impure and inhaling the pure) is an exercise in faith and enables you to continue to experience God's love and forgiveness.

1. **Exhale** — confess your sin — agree with God concerning your sin and thank Him for His forgiveness of it, according to I John 1:9 and Hebrews 10:1-25. Confession involves repentance — a change in attitude and action.

2. **Inhale** — surrender the control of your life to Christ, and appropriate (receive) the fullness of the Holy Spirit by faith. Trust that He now directs and empowers you, according to the **command** of Ephesians 5:18 and the **promise** of I John 5:14, 15.